MW00626417

NATURAL REFLECTORS

*May you find
more success
in being
less stressed.*

Jennifer Peavy

NATURAL REFLECTORS

MOVING FROM BURNOUT TO ENGAGEMENT BY PHASING REFLECTION INTO ACTION

JENNIFER PEAVEY

NEW DEGREE PRESS

COPYRIGHT © 2021 JENNIFER PEAVEY

All rights reserved.

NATURAL REFLECTORS

Moving from Burnout to Engagement by Phasing Reflection into Action

ISBN   978-1-63676-748-2 *Paperback*

             978-1-63730-493-8 *Kindle Ebook*

             978-1-63730-494-5 *Ebook*

To Lucy
for celebrating every high moment
with the joy of her wagging tail
for soothing every low moment with
the shower of her sloppy kisses

Contents

———

And Yellow decided to risk for a butterfly.
For courage she hung right beside the other
cocoon and began to spin her own.

"Imagine, I didn't even know I could do this.
That's some encouragement that I'm on the right
track. If I have inside of me stuff to make cocoons,
maybe the stuff of butterflies is there too."

— TRINA PAULUS FROM *HOPE FOR THE FLOWERS*

Introduction:
An Opening

—

"The best decisions aren't made with your mind, but with your instinct."

— LIONEL MESSI (FEARLESS MOTIVATION, 2021)

Messi is considered one of the best soccer players of all time. He has spent his entire career at the Spanish club, Barcelona, where he is presently the captain. This average-sized man consistently performs record-breaking accomplishments that have propelled him into being one of the most famous athletes in the world. His fans almost consider him a god. Who could blame them? Within his career, he has scored over seven hundred goals for club and country, achieved ten La Liga titles, including the most La Liga goals ever at four hundred forty-eight, won a record six Ballon d'Or awards and six European Golden Shoe awards, and holds the Barça club record for thirty-four trophies (FC Barcelona, 2021). His talent is so far ahead of others that some even face their losses against him by joking his ability to defy gravity proves he is not from this world.

Time and again, mere mortals have wanted to understand how he creates his magic. A simple Google search of "analysis of Messi" leads to over nine million hits, and asking him directly offers little illumination on his wizardry. In a 2009 interview with ESPN, Messi says, "I never think about the play or visualize anything. I do what comes to me at that moment. Instinct. It has always been that way" (Nielsen, 2009).

What is it that allows for Messi to create and seize such moments of instinct? The Dutch soccer legend Johan Cruyff suggests,

"[T]he secret is the speed of his change of pace; Messi changes direction every half meter. When the defense takes a step, he has taken two in two different directions. His dominion of the space-time relationship is skillful, [he] always starts first and this allows him not to be caught" (Chelala, 2015; Soccer Training Info, 2019).

We look at successful people like Messi and see them as action-focused. We assume they plan their direction and are continually driving forward in that direction, but the reality is Messi is a master of *reflection*. In a flash of a second, he takes in all the context, reflects on it, and synthesizes the information in order to act on it. He repeats again and again and again, adjusting for what he takes in and what he wants to accomplish. He repeats this process so many times and so quickly that we see it as one constant driving action he calls instinct.

We try our best to mimic these successful people by forcing our lives into a version of what we see as a constant driving action. Who could blame us for thinking this is the only way to succeed? Constant action is the core of the American dream. To keep that dream alive, Americans drive to work ever harder, longer, and faster than any other country. This American work ethic has been attributed to be the main cause of America's success. That has translated into Americans putting in thirty to ninety minutes or more per workday and four hundred more hours a year than the Germans or the Japanese (Covert, 2019).

Pressure to put in extra hours can happen at one's primary workplace, but over the last decade, there has been a rise in the number of Americans who are giving up more of their free time to second jobs or starting their own businesses. In 2019, despite unemployment being at a fifty-year low, over 43 percent of Americans reported having workload outside of their primary job. Millennials are credited with starting this trend by creating the gig economy because they were seeking additional income. The latest increase has been from Gen X-ers and Baby Boomers adopting the mindset to gain a sense of financial control late in their career and into retirement (CBS Interactive Inc., 2019).

These additional hours at work, in turn, can lead to some success in the short term, but we ultimately experience overwhelming stress in the long term. We love the taste of the success and that love blinds us to the long-term effects stress creates. We choose to believe if we hang on just a little longer, if we continue going in this way, we will finally cash in on the success we dream of.

What if the opposite were true? What
if we could be more successful if we
spent *less* of our time stressed?

There are a number of different triggers that cause stress, but
workplace stress regularly tops the list for US workers. Long
hours, heavy workloads, unclear expectations, and no control
over decision-making lead many to question their ability to
succeed in their present positions and certainly give up hope
for advancement (Casarella, 2020).

The World Health Organization's Department of Mental
Health has researched mental health in the workplace and
offers a number of resources for creating a healthy work environment. To increase productivity, WHO suggests managers
promote a sense of control and engagement, and support a
healthy work-life balance for their employees. In fact, in 2016,
they reported for every dollar invested in treating common
mental health issues, there was a four-dollar return on the
investment in productivity (World Health Organization,
2021). Yet despite the helpful resources and the proof of how
profitable taking time for mental health can be, it is still such
a common and pervasive issue that WHO has called stress
the health epidemic of the twenty-first century (Soleil, 2016).

The syndrome that results from unsuccessfully managed
chronic workplace stress is labeled as burnout. In 2019, burnout was officially classified by the World Health Organization
as an occupational phenomenon that causes people to seek
help from mental, physical, and spiritual health professionals. Three characteristics of burnout are exhaustion, lower
productivity, and putting more mental distance between

oneself and one's job (World Health Organization, 2021). In 2013, Gallop reported 70 percent of the US workforce was not engaged due to burnout (Soleil, 2016). So many people are dealing with this issue that WHO estimates it will impact the global economy by one trillion dollars every year and will cost the US alone three hundred billion dollars a year (World Health Organization, 2021; Soleil, 2016).

Burnout is bad for the economy because it is bad for us. When one is burned out and just surviving, it is almost impossible to consider what the future may hold. With more and more uncertainty, our survival can depend on our ability to see beyond today. Reflection can help. It allows us to see the past, to understand how the present was formed, and to claim the chance to create one's own future. With reflection, we can adopt a long-term view and see how our choices and actions of today can build something larger in our future.

The issue is when burned out, most people do not believe they will change. The truth is we are always reflecting on the context of the situation we are in and shifting in response. It is part of our instinct, just like Messi on the field. A 2013 study by Harvard and the University of Virginia confirms this as a blind spot for us. The research determined "people have a fundamental misconception about their future selves. Time is a powerful force that transforms people's preferences, reshapes their values, and alters their personalities, and we suspect people generally underestimate the magnitude of those changes" (Quoidbach, 2013).

With a long-term approach to life, one can consider a wide view of how systems and concepts come together and we can even take a chance to direct how the future plays out. Futurist Wendy Schultz once said,

"While the future is uncertain and much of it is beyond our control, we can control many aspects of it. We choose our future: we create it by what we do or fail to do" (Oppong, 2020).

With that in mind, are we choosing to be burned out? Is it true constant action is the best way to succeed in the long term? If not, can we shake the idea that if we aren't constantly busy, we won't succeed?

I believe we can. Once I realized Messi was including reflection to feed his actions, I wondered if I could deconstruct his process to learn more. As I dug deeper, I found Messi is not only the best in the world, but he tells us he is having "fun like a child in the street" (Fyucha, 2019). When we mimic successful people and only focus on the action portion of their lives, we tend to forget reflection cannot only make us better at what we do, but can help us enjoy it as well. If we add reflection to our actions, we will come away with a future we want to engage with and achieve results that are far more impactful. I believe it because I've seen it for myself.

As 2019 ended, I was ending nearly a decade of pushing myself to be more. The pushing began with my leaving an engineering position to seek a new one in innovation management in a new state. Within three years, I changed everything again.

I went back to college for a master's degree in industrial design in another new state. My internal drive came from the idea this was the chance to finally have my moments of instinct in my career, and in my mind that meant I would be more successful. There were some successes in the short term, but the company's long-term plans of maximizing my new skills were lost in a management shuffle, and I found myself between jobs. I decided I needed a sabbatical. I felt the need to reassess and to at least refine, if not to completely redefine, what I was doing.

This was likely the first time in a long time I had actually reflected on what I was about. That muscle was quite weak and I felt unsure and awkward. I decided to get back to the basics and see where the fundamentals led me. Throughout my career, there had been a process, and often a design process, that my colleagues and I considered a common language to help facilitate collaboration. As an engineer, I used an engineering design process that focused on solving a problem by designing, building, and testing something. In innovation, the process started with the market opportunity and nailing down the value proposition. In industrial design, the process included user research for more open-ended discovery and quick processing of information in iterations to help create focus.

As I moved to each of these different career positions, I found the inherent processes often opposed one another. I did not want to go back to any one aspect of my career, and therefore I did not want to go back to only one type of process. So, the focus of my sabbatical became a time to answer the question—what is *my* process?

I did not start with a process I knew, but with one I had never seen before. I wanted a fresh experience to guide me on my way. I was following a number of authors, such as Christine Arylo and Dr. Ezzie Spencer, who were combining modern management practices with ancient wisdom to coach women on transforming their lives (Arylo, 2021; Spencer, 2021). From these readings, I was inspired to choose what might be considered "out there" or "too feminine" to some, and I completely understand that response. I had spent much of my career following processes that emphasized action and busyness. I was seeking a more balanced approach and chose to follow a reflective practice. The phases of the moon served as a timepiece to guide me on when to gather information, when to plan, when to act, and even when to reflect. I found this cyclical nature brought a rhythm to my life.

While using the cycle, my projects did not go on forever. There were small deadlines within the cycle that encouraged me to focus versus chasing a rabbit down a hole. There were preset times for various activities that helped me know the undertaking of this phase was all I needed to do, because I could trust there was another time for anything that crossed my mind. I could place a stray thought aside and avoid the temptation of jumping on it immediately. I could also trust I would get to that thought later and not feel guilty I was adding one more thing on my list of untouched tasks. I was able to take a longer view and break large projects into smaller bites over various cycles. Working this way encouraged me with smaller successes and helped me see how each cycle was connected to successfully finish a larger accomplishment.

I would begin with forming an intent for the entire cycle, remind myself of that intent at every phase, and make decisions on the details based on that intent. I would end with a review of the entire cycle to see how it went. The time I would take could range from fifteen minutes to an hour, but I always left these moments knowing where I was, where I was going, and what I had accomplished. I made a rule of not pushing myself. In return, I felt a sense of gratitude and joy. I marveled over this, so much so that every time the gremlin inside growled I was being lazy or losing ground or would be seen as a failure if I didn't push, I actually went to battle with the gremlin to protect myself from going into burnout again. My victory was seeing more get accomplished at higher quality and enjoying myself a great deal more. When I did not reflect, I would get lost in details and slowly lose a sense of control.

The idea of this book is to explore how can we instill in our actions a mindset of intentional reflection taken from the power of nature's cycles. We can look to nature for inspiration, but like any other new thing, creating and working your own process can feel awkward. With practice, we can make it part of our approach to everything. We can shift our mindset, play the long game, and become natural reflectors.

Being inspired by nature, one can quickly see it is always adapting, and so this book will consider a number of process principles that can be readily applied and adapted to your situation. Some principles may work for you today as an employee of a corporation or firm, but tomorrow when you are a manager, it may make sense to revisit, adjust, and add a few more. You may be a creative designer who doesn't want to be confined by a process or an entrepreneur who feels a process will just distract you from the hustle of keeping afloat. The principles can also be stretched and compressed to suit the timing you give to it. Just as nature has cycles that are as short as a breath and as long as four seasons, you can apply these principles hourly, daily, monthly, or yearly.

To guide us along the way, I've collected ideas and stories from some of the greatest minds in design, authentic practitioners, and my own tumblings and triumphs. We will dive into ideas from Bill Burnett at the Stanford Life Design Lab on how we cannot make good decisions without our mind and body. We will spend some time with Stacy Levy, an environmental artist who follows nature's processes in urban environments to pull out the stories that surround each of us. We will also spend time reviewing my own times of doubt and how I struggled through to the other side in this journey.

As you begin your journey from burnt out to engaging in a life that matters to you, I want to pass on the greatest piece of advice my advisor in industrial design gave me. Anytime I was confused or struggling, she would tell me, "Jennifer, trust the process." Even when I was working through this sabbatical, she would remind me of it again. I felt quite empowered because it was one thing to trust a time-honored design process, but another entirely to trust *my* process, particularly in its infancy. She believed in me and knew I was working through the ordinary details to design my life into something special.

Trust this is your time to create your process.

PART ONE

WHERE WE ARE

ONE

The Cult of Action

"I begged him not to drink the Kool-Aid, but he did...and it was very bad."

> — TOM WOLFE, *THE ELECTRIC KOOL-AID ACID TEST* (WOLFE, 1999)

"Drink your own Kool-Aid! If you don't entirely believe in what you're doing, why should anyone else?"

> — YAEL COHEN BRAUN (WEINER, 2019)

The powdered drink mix Kool-Aid was invented in Nebraska back in the 1920s as a safe, cost-effective way to distribute a fruit drink. It was sold for ten cents a packet in six different flavors and was distributed nationally in the US by 1929. Within two years, demand grew so high the inventor, Edwin Perkins, had to drop efforts in his other products. The rationing of sugars in World War II halted further business expansion, but no one forgot about the powdered mix. After the war, the demand increased exponentially and they expanded production to a million packets a day (Hastings, 2021). Kool-Aid was a mainstay of many American childhoods for decades to come.

Being a drink mix, it was easy for people to add in their own ingredients like fresh fruit, milk, or sugar to create their own treats (Perkins Products Company, 2021). Sometimes it was taken into new realms. In 1968, Tom Wolfe wrote the non-fiction book *The Electric Kool-Aid Acid Test* that depicted the beginning of the hippie movement. One key story is about the band the Merry Pranksters, who served Kool-Aid laced with LSD (aka electric Kool-Aid) at parties in an effort to expand everyone's consciousness. This was likely the first use of the phrase "drink the Kool-Aid" (Wolfe, 1999).

Sometimes adding ingredients can be taken too far. In 1977, Jim Jones, the leader of the cult called the Peoples Temple, was paranoid about the US intelligence community and moved his church of nine hundred followers to Guyana. A number of reports of human rights violations filtered back to the US. Congressman Leo Ryan went to see for himself. As Ryan was leaving with a few defectors, Jones sent a group to stop them and, in the process, killed Ryan. As a last stand of rebellion, Jones served all of his followers a concoction of chemicals and sedatives within grape Flavor Aid (competitor to Kool-Aid). Any who tried to flee were shot, and by the end, Jones had killed over nine hundred people, including three hundred children (Higgins, 2012).

Since Kool-Aid was a household name, no one remembered Flavor Aid was used in the killing, and the phrase "drink the Kool-Aid" became a reference to death and suicide, often offending the few survivors and victims' families. It wasn't until 1984 that the phrase was used in politics to refer to blind obedience to leadership that leads to political or economic suicide (Criticism, 1984; Moore, 2013). From there, the phrase spread into corporate America, particularly in technology companies. The phrase took a turn in the late 1990s when it morphed into a neutral or even positive and inspirational connotation as an example of support and loyalty, particularly when it came to accepting the vision of a corporate leader (Moore, 2013).

Over the decades, society set aside the tragedy that caused the phrase to become mainstream, and now, since it has moved into our unconscious memory, the phrase is even considered a bit comedic (Moore, 2013; Menke, 2001). It was a slow, gradual change that can so easily happen to many other phrases, experiences, or actions in our lives. We can be so caught up in the moment we do not always realize the impact of our actions. Without focusing on the effects, we can willingly follow along and end up somewhere we didn't intend to be.

I have wondered then if this is how we wake up one day only to find ourselves burnt out. No one finishes school and starts a career with a goal of achieving burnout. Somehow, though, we walk into a situation bright and innocent, filled with dreams of how our lives will turn out, and start our new life as an "adult." Our efforts don't always work, and we decide to try a new strategy that includes watching people who seem successful from the outside.

We look for clues on how they succeeded. There may be a special parking space their shiny, new car sits in, or the way everyone else defers to them in meetings. We also see how they are working. We know they still are at work as we go home. We see e-mails from them with timestamps from the middle of the night. We decide to mimic them. Over the days, months, and years, we slowly, gradually change how we do things, thinking if we can just get one more task checked off or deciding if we dig down deep and push just a little harder, then we will see the same success. Before we know it, we are volunteering more hours than we ever agreed to when we were hired and performing jobs we never intended to do when we worked so hard in school.

This kind of life, where the system defines everything, works for some, but not for everyone. Those who attempt to flee the overwork are often seen as weak and disloyal. They may even experience their careers being killed while others who comply are promoted to more work. This is why there is so much pressure to simply go along with the status quo.

When we "drink the Kool-Aid" of overwork, it is not a joke. The truth is something in our lives is going to die. It could be that dream we had in school, it could be our health, or it could be our relationships. Whatever it is, we should take the time to make sure how we choose to spend our days is worth the loss.

THE MAKING OF A CULT

To start the examination of how we got here, it is good to understand the complexity of the system we live in. If we are going to choose to change our lives, we need to gain a perspective on the context we choose to engage with. I personally have wondered if submitting to overwork looks more like being part of a dysfunctional cult than being part of a successful, productive society. So, I researched the idea.

Janja Lalich, an expert in extremism, defines a cult as "a group or movement held together by a shared commitment to a charismatic leader or ideology. It has a belief system that has the answers to all of life's questions and offers a special solution to be gained only by following the leader's rules. It requires a high level of commitment from at least some of the members." She lists four common characteristics to all cults: a charismatic leader, a transcendent belief system, systems of control, and systems of influence (Meyer, 2016).

The charismatic leader starts the group with a message that resonates with a few followers who then spread that message, creating a tone that centers around the leader. The group's belief is by taking part, the members will move to a better place by going through a required transformation. Along the path of transformation, there are increasing systems of rules and regulations modeled by senior members of the cult that create influence and control over the group. Members are completely immersed in this new reality and their minds are closed to any other worldview. The cult becomes the only source of light and hope (Meyer, 2016).

If we examine constant action as a cult, are these four characteristics present? Is there a cult of action?

THE CHARACTERISTICS OF THE CULT OF ACTION

America is seen as a land of opportunity. If one is willing to work hard, then one can achieve anything. While there is not a particular charismatic leader at the center, the ideology that hard work is the only way to live is pervasive in American corporate culture and suggests the first cult characteristic. I agree work is required to see and maintain success. I wonder, though, if there is a line that constant action crosses to either make us isolate ourselves from being productive or leads us to killing everything we hold dear.

If hard work was the only thing needed to succeed, why is there a 366-billion-dollar industry for business leadership development (Westfall, 2019)? It is because those in leadership positions search for ways to transform their organizations to be more effective and consume nearly everything this industry produces in an effort to make their companies more successful. Here could be the second cult characteristic: a transcendent belief system.

The issue is the advice on how to be more effective can also make an organization less successful. Yet, the belief system is so strong, organizations can miss the negative side effects of implementing the advice. Award-winning leadership thinker Jeffrey Pfeffer dissects the industry in his book *Leadership BS*, seeking to uncover why despite the intent to lead well, business leadership development is resulting in employee disengagement, high turnover rates, and failed development efforts (Pfeffer, 2015).

Among a number of points in his research, two particularly stood out that show a large disconnect between leadership and employees. The first is the idea that while those in leadership have a lot of responsibility, they have less stress because they are in control of what they do and how they do it. Those who follow have less, if any, control. "One of the most stressful things is to have a lot of job demands but no control over how and when you meet those job demands." Leaders make decisions that affect the employees without knowing or sometimes caring what is really happening throughout the organization. One such example of this disconnect is leaders who felt working hard or being loyal deserved nothing more than a regular paycheck (UNSW Business School, 2014).

Leadership is ultimately responsible for how the organization performs and will need to make decisions for the good of the company. Those decisions will affect individuals in different ways. This is part of the stress of leadership. When the company culture moves from a healthy, supportive organization where employees are valued to a controlling organization where employees are considered objects, it could be indicative of the third cult characteristic: systems of control.

Another disconnect between leadership and employees that Pfeffer identifies is while the leadership industry preaches the need for transparency and honesty, successful leaders are not always either or both. Pfeffer asserts the leadership industry spreads myths about business leaders as heroes or knights in shining armor. For example, the famous CEO of GE, Jack Welch, is described as valuing every employee and inspiring confidence. These stories became what corporate employees expect to receive in their leadership. Pfeffer's research shows the successful business leaders are far more flawed. Welch frequently used a "rank and yank" policy where the bottom

10 percent would be fired as a matter of course, regardless of overall performance, to manage costs. This policy resulted in an aggressive internal culture to survive (UNSW Business School, 2014).

Again, leadership must make difficult decisions that influence the company culture. Positive or negative, the policies and procedures that are developed influence employee behavior. When the results foster collaboration, innovation, and positive energy, employees are more engaged. Yet, even the most positively written policies can create turmoil in a company culture when employees use them to manipulate and control others. This could be an indication of the fourth cult characteristic: systems of influence.

> "The land of opportunity spawned a whole
> new breed of men without souls."
>
> — DON HENLEY (DON HENLEY, 2021)

This behavior can also be less obvious and something everyone has done. Pfeffer tells of a story where over many months, a good friend had to slowly watch his daughter die after a drug overdose. His employer was sympathetic for a couple of weeks, but eventually he was expected to get back to the job he was hired for. His employees may have been sympathetic for a couple more weeks, but they also expected him to place the pain aside and be fully present in an engaged, energetic way. To continue to be a leader, one is often asked to betray their authenticity to put the group's needs ahead of their own (Talks at Google, 2015). In doing this, they model a behavior that makes it very easy for the employees to feel they should give up a day on the weekend to complete work or pull an all-nighter to get ready for that presentation. When this is a one-off, it might be considered tolerable, but when it becomes the norm, burnout is not far behind.

When looking at the four characteristics of a cult, we can see how some corporate cultures mimic a cult. There is a created system where the leadership is divine with a mythical aura and we have a leadership industry creating a tone centered around that divinity. There is at least anecdotal evidence of the systems of control and influence. Business cultures can become machines who promote a cult of action that eventually leads to employee burnout. What can we do if we want to defect? Pfeffer suggests if we can realistically see the flaws in our leadership and regard the people in those positions as humans, we can also see ourselves as human. In turn, we can accept ourselves and adopt behaviors that allow us to function in the system *and* take us where we want to go (Talks at Google, 2015).

THE EFFECTIVENESS OF BUSY

If we can agree there is a cult of action, we then have the choice of joining or not. For me to decide, I want to examine whether the cult is effective. Is this the best or only way of accomplishing tasks and taking us where we want to go? To do so, I went back to my education in industrial design and researched how humans work. My hope was the results would give me insights into how methods were chosen and how effective they were.

Industrial designers often call observing, understanding, and accepting the reality in humans to be a form of empathy. By going through the process of questioning the human condition from different perspectives, designers are then able to gain insights that lead to breakthrough innovations. This happens not only because the innovation meets the needs of the real human with new materials or technologies, but through this acknowledgment of the human condition, there is often faster acceptance of the innovation by the real humans, because they feel heard and understood by the designer or company. This feeling of being understood leads to fierce loyalty, a more secure following, and even free viral word of mouth advertising.

To dive deeper into this, I talked with Dr. Andres Tellez, who researched empathetic development in industrial design students at Jorge Tadeo Lozano University in Bogotá, Colombia. I had hoped to hear about the tension that comes from encouraging designers to take the time to gain this empathy prior to acting. It came as a surprise that we actually talked more about self-compassion.

Andres had enjoyed working with the students in the classroom. Then, in 2020, he saw the opportunity to step up and applied to become the department head. In August, he received the position. Overnight, his schedule completely changed. His time was not his own anymore. He started working twelve to sixteen hours a day and became completely exhausted.

This situation came from the need to keep the university open. This private university was designed and staffed for fourteen thousand students and was gradually losing the student population each year to a 2020 level below fifty percent. Pressure was put on the administration to find ways to run more efficiently and explore new funding sources. At the same time, the department was under an accreditation review that was behind schedule. Andres had certain expectations of making profound changes in the department to improve the educational experience, but reality was with the financial stress—the program was simply trying to survive. He ended his story with,

> "I feel like I'm in a hurricane, in the middle of an earthquake. It's very, *very* stressful."

With the global pandemic in 2020, working from home with his family on the other side of the wall was a new, huge tension. The hardest part was his seven-year-old daughter telling him, "I am bored of you not having time for me." He looked at me across the video call and admitted he did not have the answer. "I wish I had come up with a very smart and designed way to overcome these difficulties, but I haven't and I really don't know if that is possible because of my current position."

It wasn't for the lack of trying, but there was not a moment for any of them to decompress. "We're here twenty-four seven, and it's like we put all that we usually used to do into a blender. Now everything is mixed in some kind of medium." Andres wanted to be stable for his family, so he did manage to consider strategies on how to have more time for them and for himself, but before he could even start, he became sick.

At first, he didn't know the sore throat was more than just talking too much on video calls. The following weekend, a cough started to develop. His sister had come to visit earlier in the week. He wondered if she may have had COVID and was asymptomatic. By Sunday night, he not only felt bad physically, but the mental anxiety was building. His doctor ordered a COVID test that would take two days for the results to come back.

On Monday, Andres did not attend meetings to allow himself some flexibility, but he did answer over four hundred e-mails that awaited him. As the day went on, he was only getting sicker and he realized his body was telling him to stop. He fortunately listened and started up *The Queen's Gambit* on Netflix. One scene that stuck with him was where the talented chess player was competing with twelve people at the same time, going from one board to another. He realized that was how he felt at work. There were many rooms full of people with different chessboards, and he had to strategically respond to every one of those boards. There was no team. As an administrator, he played these matches in isolation. The metaphor helped him see that was not what he wanted. He did not get a PhD for doing this.

Fortunately, the COVID test was negative. As he continued to recover, he chose to make some changes. First, he made breakfast in the morning for the whole family. It had become his meditation time and it helped because it was one activity where he felt he was in full control. He had found a moment of peace in the middle of that craziness. On the weekends, the family had a movie night where Andres admitted he often fell asleep before the ending because he felt safe at home.

The biggest change Andres chose was to be faithful to his convictions about modern empathy and to understand his own human limitations. He left that position and the university, seeking a more balanced life where he could have time for his family and his own personal and spiritual growth. He started a new teaching position at Appalachian State University in North Carolina, where he returned to working with students, with an emphasis on empathetic design.

Much like Andres, it is easy for us to become immersed in the new reality of our busyness and close our minds to any other view. Often against our choosing, we hit a brick wall, such as getting sick, that causes us to suddenly stop. In those moments, looking back at the situation, was the workload effective? Will the effort take us where we want to go?

In the cases where it did not, it is my hope we see being part of the cult of action is a choice.

In that moment, we can choose to extend some self-compassion to let ourselves be human and rest, to seek a moment of peace in breakfast, and to fall asleep in front of a movie because we feel at home. But mostly, I hope we can make changes that allow us to use our talents for what we are truly passionate about. For in that, we will be the most effective we can be.

HUMAN VERSUS MACHINE

What is in the ideology of the cult of action that makes us ignore the signs we are heading toward burnout? How do we celebrate busy for busyness' sake? Why do we fear slowing down? Is it the potential loss of our positions, our status, and ultimately our money? Who exactly would we be losing all of this to? Is it that we think we are competing with machines and the only way to win is to be a machine?

There is a history of machines replacing human labor, such as the cotton gin (Kelly, 2019). There are even stories of humans competing directly with machines, such as John Henry and the steam drill or the IBM computer Watson competing on the American trivia game show *Jeopardy!* (National Park Service, 2021; Robot Workforce, 2013). With the age of artificial intelligence, we are not only being replaced physically, but mentally. In 2015, a study from Oxford University predicted in twenty years, half the human workforce will be replaced by computers in an effort to increase efficiency and profits (Frey, 2017).

Tim Leberecht, a business romantic, explores the idea of creating organizations that maintain humanity in the age of machines in his 2016 TEDSummit Talk. "Because as machines take our jobs and do them more efficiently, soon the only work left for us humans will be the kind of work that must be done beautifully rather than efficiently."

One of the principles he introduces to create beautiful organizations is to do the unnecessary. He recalls a story of an attempt to unify an IT outsourcing firm and a small design firm by creating a third new brand entity. At the launch, ten thousand orange balloons were to be distributed to all of the staff worldwide. In an effort to save money, the balloon idea was cut. Unifying the two cultures failed miserably. Leberecht does not blame the lack of balloons, but the "kill-the-balloons mentality" that became the standard for everything else (TED, 2016).

> "You might not always realize it, but when you cut the unnecessary, you cut everything."
>
> — TIM LEBERECHT, FOUNDER AND CEO AT
> HOUSE OF BEAUTIFUL BUSINESS

I thought this was a heart-warming story, but I really wasn't sure how real it was until it happened to me.

In 2017, I moved into a house that had private outdoor space and a fenced-in backyard. This was for me and my dear black Labrador, Lucy. I had spent four years walking dogs four times a day while living in a high-rise of condos. I was done with that. The flip side is I am not good with maintenance, so mowing a lawn was not something I would keep up with. I decided with a dog and plant-killing poop, the best thing would be to minimize the grass and mulch everything else.

In 2020, during the pandemic, I adopted a mindset of minimizing costs, so I took on the mulch spreading. In North Carolina, it took until May before the twenty yards of mulch was delivered. Most of my neighbors found the whole situation entertaining and I let them laugh. I actually appreciated being outside working in the mornings. But in July, when the temperatures started to match the humidity, I was looking forward to the end of this project. By the time I would finish the day's allotment of spreading, I would be drenched in sweat. I really had no idea the cumulative effect that was having on me. So, in hindsight, I know I was not prepared for the night the smoke alarm went off and my dear Lucy panicked.

Years earlier, when I was in the condo with two black Labs, Shadow and Raven, the complex had a centralized industrial fire alarm system. When it went off, the sound was so loud, it would drive you to go outside. The dogs would physically push me to do something, anything about the horrific noise. I would scramble to dress both in their harnesses while they squirmed and squealed. When I could finally open the door to the condo, it was all I could do to keep them from dragging me down the hall.

This "must-do-something-now" reaction was ingrained in my every nerve. So that night, as the house alarm went off and Lucy panicked, I automatically kicked into pushing mode. The first thing I did was open the back door so Lucy could get away from the sound. About that time, the alarm stopped, so she stayed with me. I knew it would likely sound again before I changed the battery. I went to the other side of the kitchen to fetch earplugs.

As I put the earplugs in my hands, I could feel my head swooning. I must have gotten up too quickly, and I took a moment to let my head clear. Lucy kept pressing my legs in her panic, so I obliged by turning around to go back toward the bedroom. What happened from there is a bit muddled. I remember this dreamlike state of my head plummeting facedown. I consciously thought, *I have a concussion; I need to get to the floor and put my feet up.*

When I came to, I was alone in the dark and the silence. I had no idea how long I had lain in the middle of the kitchen floor. As I slowly grew conscious, I dragged my tongue across my teeth and knew something wasn't right. I reached a hand up to check for blood. There was none. I stood up in disbelief, walked over to the counter, and flipped the light switch on. As I squinted at the counter, I found there the shattered fragments of my two front teeth.

It was not a big deal to change the battery in the smoke alarm, and Lucy did come back inside after some coaxing. My teeth, though, were permanently gone. There are a thousand things I could blame for the loss, but the ultimate reason is I chose to push at a time when I was clearly not able to do any more. I had taken the mindset of cutting everything unnecessary from my spending and applied the same rigidity to solving the problem of the smoke alarm. Just as the IT firm was unaware of how pervasive the mindset of cutting the balloons would be, I adopted a closed way of thinking that focused on what couldn't be. There was no room to consider if there were other options. Because of that, I broke my teeth and all that goes with it.

Teeth are repairable and I can adjust to new ways of eating. Much worse could have happened. The experience makes me truly consider how human I am and the permanency of decisions. I now want to think of ways to set myself up better.

We are all products of what we think and believe. Actions from those thoughts and beliefs can be powerful or powerless depending on what thoughts and beliefs we choose to let in. When we choose to listen to and believe the cult of action, we move from being productive to being busy for busyness' sake. We then enter into a space where we work to keep the machine running and may even look at ourselves as just another machine.

> Leaving the cult can be difficult and
> even devastating, but it is our chance
> to emerge beautifully human.

TWO

Natural Reflection

———

"To ferment your own food is also a declaration of independence from an economy that would much prefer we remain passive consumers of its standardized commodities, rather than creators of idiosyncratic products expressive of ourselves and of the places where we live, because your pale ale or sourdough bread or kimchi is going to taste nothing like mine or anyone else's."

— MICHAEL POLLAN, *COOKED: A NATURAL HISTORY OF TRANSFORMATION* (POLLEN, 2013)

Kimchi is a side dish of fermented vegetables that can be found at every meal served in Korea whether it is at home or in a restaurant. It is considered extremely important to the nation's culinary traditions, much like how one would think of bread as part of French cuisine, rice as part of Chinese, and pasta as part of Italian.

It has been eaten in Korea since the thirteenth century as they borrowed salt preservation methods from northern China, but it wasn't until the sixteenth century when hot peppers were introduced to Korea that kimchi took on its heat. Kimchi was created to ensure the harvest did not go to waste and there would be plenty for everyone to eat through the winter. Today, kimchi is prepared for the sake of having kimchi, but the tradition still focuses on harvesting and preservation.

There are literally hundreds of different kinds of kimchi that vary due to the vegetables that are harvested. Even within a region, the kimchi can be customized by other ingredients, like salted fish, or how long the concoction is allowed to ferment (Chin, 2009). I imagine even within the family, there can be variations from year to year depending on who is helping out in the kitchen or how the cooks are feeling.

In any case, the common part of the recipe is to slice the vegetables, often cabbage, into a large bowl. Let this stand in salt water overnight. Next, drain and massage the softened vegetables with a spicy paste, then pack into airtight containers and leave the kimchi alone to ferment. The container can be left out at room temperature for a few days and/or in the fridge to slow down the process (Ford, 2021).

Kimchi is an outcome from harvesting a number of beautiful things and creating an environment where something wonderful can happen. The most crucial steps in the making are the ones in which you pause, let the magic happen, and leave it be before doing anything else with it. Without these, it is not kimchi.

If kimchi comes only from including moments of rest, then when we are creating something, are there not situations where it is crucial to also include periods where we pause as part of a recipe for success?

> To develop a process that brings our life purpose, we then should intentionally create an environment where we encourage moments of reflection.

WHAT IT MEANS TO REFLECT

Reflection is not just for monks and sages, and it is not just a luxury when we take a vacation. Reflection is actually something that improves the quality of our decisions, just as it improves the quality of the kimchi.

In his TEDxStanford Talk, the executive director of the Stanford Design Program, Bill Burnett, told the audience we could not choose well if we chose only from our rational mind. He followed his statement up with a study of grocery shoppers presented with a selection of jams to taste. One day, there were only six jams, and another, there were twenty-four. On the day of twenty-four, twice as many people stopped to taste the jams, but fewer people made a purchase. The shoppers went into choice overload and the result was not making a choice.

Psychologists advise by reducing the number of selections down to five, a person will be able to make a choice. The issue is when we know there are more options not considered, we will fear we have made the wrong choice. What if we eliminated the right one?

The quality of our decisions or the perception of "right" and "wrong" is about how we *feel* about the selections available, not what we logically think about the choice (TEDx Talks, 2017).

Burnett goes on to talk of Daniel Goleman's research in emotional intelligence. It turns out part of the brain—the basal ganglia—is responsible for providing us with a summary of our emotions. It is not connected to the prefrontal cortex where conscious thoughts emerge. The basal ganglia are connected to the gastrointestinal tract and the limbic system. It sends that summary of emotions through physical sensations, and this is what we call feeling with your gut (Goleman, 1995). Without listening to the gut, we do not know if our decisions are good or not.

This concept is not just for decisions, but also can be applied to how we create and innovate. Terri Trespicio, a former magazine editor and radio host at Martha Stewart, touched on this as she advised me on how to think about my writing. She pressed the idea writing is actually a whole-body experience, because one cannot think without the body. "How would you know if something was fuzzy or very clear, or sharp or warm or tight? All of that is body language. The kind of writing that will move audiences is going to come from your body, not from your brain."

For most of us in the modern digital world, this can seem foreign. This is why the idea of intentional reflection is so needed. A moment to pause can allow us to hear from our gut about the quality of our decisions. If we are not well-versed in the language of our body, then we may need to slow down so we can understand it. This can require time, practice, and immersion, just like learning any foreign language.

If intentional reflection is so needed, why is it so difficult for us to take the time to do it? Carl Honoré presents some answers in his TEDGlobal Talk, "In Praise of Slowness." He drills down looking for the core driver on why the world has become so accelerated. He talks of urbanization, consumerism, the workplace, and the use of technology, but these are context and tools. Honoré submits our behavior is driven by how we think about time.

"In the West, time is linear. It's a finite resource; it's always draining away. You either use it or lose it." Because of the feeling of loss, we speed up to "turn every moment of every day into a race to the finish line" (Honoré, 2005).

Racing through our days causes us to feel action is our only choice, and we do not see a time of reflection as valuable to us.

There is an alternative. "In other cultures, time is cyclical. It's seen as moving in great, unhurried circles. It's always renewing and refreshing itself" (Honoré, 2005). If we consider this alternative, then we can see we are not losing anything by slowing down for a time of reflection. If we listen to Burnett, Goleman, and Trespicio, the opposite is true; we actually lose by not slowing down. When the time of reflection is used well, it will allow us to evaluate if the options before us are even the right ones to be considering, and when we like our options, we achieve higher quality decisions. It would then make sense we would want to intentionally create space for reflection in the processes we develop so we can make better lives for ourselves.

BEHIND THE SCENES OF SLOWING DOWN

The prospect of slowing down can be counterintuitive when we have been indoctrinated into the cult of action. In fact, it may feel as if we are divorcing from everything we have ever been taught and heading toward certain failure. Still, if it is necessary to create our best work and best selves, it is something worth trying. To help battle the gremlin who says, "Don't you dare slow down!" it is good to take a look at what healthy slowing down looks like.

Let's go back to the kimchi. Say you've made a batch and are now waiting for it to be ready to serve at dinner. We say it is fermenting, but what does that actually mean? The specific process is lacto-fermentation, where lactic acid bacteria break down the carbohydrates in the vegetables into lactic acid and carbon dioxide.

Sounds a bit like rotting vegetables, doesn't it? *The Noma Guide to Fermentation* describes rotting and fermentation to be as different as an unsavory dive versus a happening nightclub. "[Rotting] is a club where everyone gets in: bacteria and fungi, safe or unsafe, flavor enhancing or destructive. [Whereas in fermentation], you're taking on the role of a bouncer, keeping out unwanted microbes and letting in the ones that are going to make the party pop" (Baechu Kimchi, 2021).

The bouncer for making kimchi is the salt water that the vegetables sit in overnight. The salt breaks through the walls of the harmful pathogens, like Salmonella, and the submersion kills the oxygen-loving pathogens that create mold. The lactic acid bacteria start to feast on the vegetables, releasing acid to lower the pH and keep other pathogens, like botulism, from growing. The party keeps going until all the carbohydrates are gone and the kimchi turns to vinegar. The whole point is to preserve the vegetables and make the kimchi safe to eat and easier for the body to absorb (Baechu Kimchi, 2021).

From the outside, it can look like there is nothing going on while the kimchi is "pausing." The fact is, though, there is much going on at a level that is generally not seen. The process must be trusted to achieve the outcome of kimchi.

Dr. Byungsoo Kim helped me see how the pause in the process of making kimchi can act as a metaphor for using reflection in our own processes. Byungsoo is a professor of industrial design at Kansas State University and has spent time not only working on projects for clients and himself, but guiding students in navigating the design process as well.

When I think of the design process, I think of what is often called the Double Diamond process that was popularized by the British Design Council in the mid-2000s (British Design

Council, 2007). The visual for the process is two diamonds that are laid next to each other. The intention is as you go through this process, there are times of divergence and times of convergence. The first diamond focuses on defining the problem and the second on finding the solution. Each diamond has a divergent and a convergent phase. Often the design process is described as four phases: *discover* insights into the problem, *define* the scope of the problem solution, *develop* potential solutions, and *deliver* the final solution (Middleton, 2019).

With this definition in mind, I asked Byungsoo about his insights on how reflection was used within the design process and found it interesting how the definition of reflection evolved.

Byungsoo liked to begin by sitting with an idea.

> "When I have some interesting design idea in my head, I know when I have it…[it will be] sitting there for a certain amount of time… In Korea, there is a food called kimchi and… when you put it in the refrigerator, the taste gets better. For me, it is a similar process."

He told me of one project that started very conceptually. He was playing with the idea of contrast and how a product may contain opposites. In his reading, he latched onto the idea of creating a product design that had the concept of life and death together. This tension was interesting to him. He kept his eye out for products that held the concept and wasn't readily finding them. After a while, he moved on to other things. The fall came and while taking a walk, he noticed the leaves at the base of a tree. He was reminded of the concept and wondered if he could make a pot out of dead leaves that could hold a live plant.

In this project, Byungsoo did not rush to make a final product. He explored materials, knowing the leaves would need structure to be formed. He kept his eye out for biodegradable materials and did not readily find what he wanted. Before he knew it, summer had come. The flowers were saturated with colors that excited him. He gathered them to make a powder he mixed with glue to explore the colors and textures.

While interesting, this information was not gelling for him, so he was not ready to consider shape. Without a pull toward form, he could not see a reason to sketch and ideate. He explained, "I feel the knowledge that is in my brain is not enough to generate ideas…My brain is kind of a glass, and I'm pouring water [into it], and if it is full and is floating out, then I think that's the time I start to take action. When the glass is full, I naturally try to do [something]."

The knowledge was also curated, much like the bad pathogens are removed from the kimchi. The accumulation of years of experience in his craft helped him to know, in his gut, what information was worth keeping on this project. It was a whole-body decision, so it was hard for him to articulate. However, he knew not only when he had enough information, but also when the information supported creating the right aesthetic, the right form, and the right amount of innovation.

He also knew what part was not ready to move forward with and returned to researching with a more focused view.

Byungsoo enjoyed this project and was readily motivated to work on it. I wondered aloud if he might be able to teach phases of reflection to students to make their work more enjoyable. This was where we started to expand the definition of reflection.

We considered his students learning how to design. The concepts and ideas in a design project come from data from personal experience or research. Reflection can be helpful when looking back to see what they have done to understand the story they will tell about the design. Byungsoo liked for the students to have a glass at least half-full to have something to play with as they reflected. In this case, reflection can be about receiving, collecting, and sorting through techniques such as journaling, talking through it with others, or sleeping on it.

Later in the project, the students may be ideating or even prototyping. In these times, it is easy to be caught up in the details. Reflection can help them go back to the data and make sure something has not been missed. He commented it is easy to overlook insights. Even after leaving college, he would catch himself running a project without looking back at what had been accomplished. In this case, reflection could be intentionally taking breaks from the work and coming back with fresh eyes. One could then use a checklist or a project review to ensure nothing important was missed.

For any case or definition, the moments of reflection can be seen as not generating anything and could be readily discarded in the drive to be busy. Much like the kimchi, the behind the scenes effort is often the key to making the project successful. It is good then when we develop our process to have steps where we start with a clean, empty glass and take the time to fill it up so when we act, we will be able to use our intuition along with our logic to make better decisions.

THE BENEFITS OF REFLECTION

What could happen if we slow down and trust the process? Slowing down can allow us to reflect, and if we trust the process in those moments, we are setting ourselves up for making higher quality decisions.

Research has shown we not only know the quality of our decisions, but the rested mind is able to handle problems more creatively and solve more complex problems (Baird, 2012; Dijksterhuis, 2006). It turns out in the reflective periods, the brain moves to an internal processing mode that is suppressed when we are externally focused. Regularly exercising the internally focused mode increases reading comprehension and divergent thinking (Immordino-Yang, 2012).

If we take this further, like becoming an expert, there is other research that shows the elite among us actually spend less time practicing than the average. After about ten years of deliberate effort, there is a shift that allows those becoming elite to have more focus when they are "on." To do so, they require having "off" times that allow for recovery (Ericcson et. al., 1993).

Take a cellist. The goal of a beginner is to get to know the instrument and work on getting the notes correct. As one advances, time with the cello is about learning how the practice can be more efficient so you can maximize the time spent. For the elite, the practice is about the interpretation of the music. The elites already know the mechanics and the process that works best for them. They are now working that process. The time "off" the instrument is about researching the score, understanding the composer's intent, investigating how others have performed the piece, and planning how this performance will be authentic to the cellist (Moore, 2021).

In 2016, Yo-Yo Ma spoke to a group at the New England Conservatory of Music about his practice. Once he has the concept of how he wants to perform the music, he goes to the cello to try it. He then reflects on how it went.

"Whenever I don't feel at ease, I can tell. Let's try and make it secure so the mind is free to…make choices at the time they're performing. You're free to respond to anything that comes your way, so you can actually have a conversation with the orchestra and the conductor. It's freedom in the mind, so you can physically do whatever you need to do. I think that's really why we practice" (CelloBello, 2017).

We need to give ourselves moments and experiences that will allow us to perform well when we are called upon. We readily expect a recovery period for professionals so they will perform better at a concert or on game day. We often don't grant the same idea to ourselves when we prepare and face our own mental performance days.

What if we did approach our lives that way? What if we looked at what we did today as if it was in preparation for a big game? Would we not want to follow a regime that included moments of intentional reflection to recover and assess how things were progressing?

I have been working with this concept in the development of my own process. I knew from personality tests that my intuition is rather strong and my sources of joy were making and creating. To maximize these, I could see the need for reflection to let my intuition have its moment.

I looked for inspiration from Christine Arylo and Dr. Ezzie Spencer and took their advice to consider the phases of the moon (Arylo, 2021; Spencer, 2021). Since the moon is always there, I felt it would be a constant reminder as I started a new habit. My other thought was a twenty-nine-day moon cycle was a long enough period of time to test ideas thoroughly and a short enough bite of time to have some movement. With all this in mind, I developed a process where the phases of the moon became a timepiece to tell me when to gather information, when to plan, when to act, and even when to reflect.

I tested my new process with the next moon cycle and journaled to document how things were going. As I read back, there were some interesting moments of insight. For example, I've never been good at maintenance and often toss tasks aside by saying, "I don't do maintenance." One emphasis for the year was self-care, so I decided to care for my skin by lathering it with lotion, something I would never be bothered to do in the past.

In the journal, I wrote, "Putting on lotion is a sign of love." I expanded the thought from there. Cleaning the bathroom is a sign of love. Organizing a closet is a sign of love. *Maintenance* is a sign of love. I won't say this insight has made me better at maintenance. I still get easily distracted, but this moment of insight showed me maintenance is not something to look at as drudgery. Therefore, when I am not so distracted, I am more motivated to do maintenance.

Cleaning one bathroom once a month is certainly not a complex mental task and not a game day activity, but I could see how reflection can create a mental shift to make the small tasks of today support or build to those elite skills. I found as I continued through the phases, I watched for more insights like these.

When I reached a moon phase full of action, I kept a to-do list. To-do lists sometimes work for me and sometimes don't. In reflecting, I realized that is because there are phases of action where they are helpful, but in phases of reflection, they are not. I thought that was interesting and quickly moved on to the next task on the to-do list.

At a later moon phase, I was feeling very tense and I was not sure where the tension was coming from. I journaled I needed to create a retreat for this phase. I realized this was a time to review all that had happened, to sit with a wall of post-it notes, and to synthesize the findings. Suddenly, my mind opened and I could see something much bigger.

Gleaning information, placing tidbits on post-its, sorting through, rearranging them, and living with them is a core method I use when I am working a design project. It is a moment for me in the middle of the design process where I pull all the research together and look for insights that will be translated into design criteria when I move to work on solutions. Connecting the idea of using post-its anchored my mind between the "old" design process and my "new" moon cycle process.

With that tether between these two mental worlds, I could see what I was attempting was actually the design process with the moon phases as a timepiece. I recalled the earlier insight that there are times for to-do lists and times for freedom from to-do lists. My instinct told me I was looking at something new. Over the next few days of living with the post-its, the vision morphed and I could see there was a cycle to when all of the tasks would be applied or not. A better definition of the purpose of the phases formed. I could see the phases in a cycle were moving back and forth through a continuum of generating to receiving, focused to flexible, small steps to large strides, and an overview to details.

My new process began to feel like breathing to me. It was now nourishing and cleansing, productive and energizing.

Without reflecting back on what had happened, all of these visions would have been lost and developing my own process would have been abandoned as another bit of maintenance. Reflection allowed me to sit with the ideas and let them ferment. I could then see the significance of the small details and how they fit together into a larger whole. The vision of that larger whole is something that resonated with me and my gut declared, "It is good!" Logic could then take over to determine, plan, and create to-do lists. My soul could find its peace knowing what I was working on mattered.

THREE

Can Reflection and Action Coexist?

———

"God turns you from one feeling to another and teaches by means of opposites so you will have two wings to fly, not one."

— RUMI (RUMI, 1996)

Laughter has been called great medicine. There is more data every year that defines how positive laughter can be in our lives. The Mayo Clinic reports there are short-term and long-term benefits. In the short term, laughing relieves stress by increasing our intake of oxygen to stimulate the heart, lungs, and muscles that in turn trigger our brain to release endorphins. The act of laughter suddenly increases our heart rate and blood pressure, which stimulates circulation throughout the body. Afterward, the decrease in heart rate and blood pressure causes the muscles to let go, giving us a good, relaxed feeling.

In the long term, the body will release natural painkillers more often. The additional release of stress helps our moods, our desire to connect with others, and our ability to cope with hard times. We are able to have more positive thoughts overall, which triggers the brain to release chemical signals that further prevent stress and support our immune system (Mayo Clinic, 2021).

It seems laughter is an important component to staving off burnout. So, why do people laugh and what does it take to make us laugh? From the body's perspective, laughter is a release of our emotions. One common way to make people laugh is to tell a joke. The key to telling a joke people laugh at is to build anticipation that is suddenly released by a surprise (Lee, 2021). A good comedian will have his audience sitting upright and leaning in to see what is going to happen next. This is stressful and people pay good money to be stressed like this because of the surprise that leads to the release.

Look at a classic example.

> ## "Outside of a dog, a book is a man's best friend. Inside of a dog, it's too dark to read."
> — GROUCHO MARX (LARKIN, 2018)

Even with just a few words, a talented comedian leaves us wondering where they are going. Just as we settle in to follow them, the joke surprises us with a mental twist. I find my imagination continues the enjoyment by living the story they've created. I can feel how cramped I would be inside of a dog and how ridiculous it is to try to read in the dark. The comedian literally casts me into the water with the line and I am in another world. That moment of imagination is what makes the joke stick in my memory, has me laughing days later, and extends those long-term health benefits.

Laughter is a combination of opposites that creates an experience we desire. Without the tension, we will not pay attention, and without the surprise, we will not laugh and release the tension. As we look to develop our own processes, it is good to look for opposites that will help us create strong methods to keep us engaged but also bring us joy. Often our culture considers reflection and action to be opposites that do not go together, but just as one cannot have laughter without tension, our actions are not strong in the long term unless there is reflection.

PUTTING TOGETHER REFLECTION AND ACTION

In 2020, fate presented me with this notion of combining reflection and action as I was in the middle of exploring the idea of "developing my own process." While I worked my projects through the new process, I often felt the need to check how things were going. I experimented with different ways of collecting and processing information. One project involved developing a product, and I observed what kind of insights I could learn from various resolutions of prototypes. Sometimes my gut would tell me something was not quite right, prompting me to stop and consider why I felt this way.

At one point, I created a number of prototypes of the product concept, reviewed their performance, and collected insights from the effort. As I finished, the thought crossed my mind—what now? I realized when the project had a client, I would present to them where we were and solicit feedback.

In this particular project, I was the client. So, awkwardly, I prepared a presentation I gave to my imaginary client-self sitting across the table. At the end, I literally asked for any questions or comments. After a pause, I mentally switched to becoming the client. I gave myself the feedback I always gave others, the feedback I had never given to myself because I was too close to the project. I realized suddenly how powerful this method was. It was an epiphany on what it means to reflect on my prior actions.

I often shared epiphanies with a friend of mine who enjoyed watching me on this journey. She always encouraged me and I was grateful for it. Then came the moment I suggested she try some of this for her work.

"That's not realistic" was the response.

I let it go, but I wondered to myself if there was a way for pausing to be something that coexists with the hard driving action. Pushing was a large part of my life before 2020. Reflection and action coexisting had become important to me. After 2020, there would be a time for me to "go back to work" and I did not want to lose everything I had gained.

So, I started my quest. How could reflection and action coexist in the same process?

I did find research on a number of ways of bringing reflection and action together. Researchers have called this a reflective practice where a need or experience triggers one to explore what has happened in the past and everyone's role in what happened. A comprehensive exploration can identify how one might change the approach for a future event (La Trobe University, 2021). An exploration would require an openness to analysis, problem-solving, learning by doing, and critical thinking (Edwards, 1999).

Reflecting on the past is not the only type of reflective practice. Researchers describe three separate ways of integrating reflection and action: reflection *before* the event (reflection-for-action), reflecting *during* the event (reflection-in-action), and reflecting *after* an event (reflection-on-action) (Olteanu, 2017).

No matter one's situation or type of work, there is likely a benefit, even if the term "reflective practice" is not used. A number of professions, such as education, do call on reflective practice to improve the performance of their employees (Stearns-Pfeiffer, 2011). The reliance requires trust in the individual to take the time to reflect, so leadership often encourages employees through methods, procedures, and space to ensure the employees do not forget to reflect and slip in their performance.

In one research study, Dr. Geoffrey Wright sought to make reflection easier and more effective for educators. He developed an innovative process using digital video to encourage teachers to reflect. The teachers used a baseline method where they identified skills that needed improvement, selected one of the skills and timing to apply it, taught the new skill, and filled out a form to guide their reflection. Wright then included a video of their teaching moment to compare with the baseline.

Prior to participating in the study, a survey showed three-quarters of the teachers knew about reflective practice from their college education. All of them believed they were fairly reflective, but only 60 percent admitted having an informal reflection practice where they included short notes with the lesson plan. All of the teachers appreciated the guided reflection format and felt the reflection was far more effective than their informal practice.

While they enjoyed the form that prompted them to put their thoughts on paper, the teachers felt supplementing the writing exercise with the video or only using the video was more informative. This was evident in the fact there were twice as many reflective comments from the video session than the writing session. Analysis of the comments showed the difference was not just in the volume, but the breadth and depth of the comments. The teachers were able to identify more skills that needed improvement and became more aware of how the skills were interconnected (Wright, 2010).

Wright's research does not show whether the teachers adopted the methods from the study permanently, but he does say encouragement from the principal and having a support group of other teachers did encourage them to not only use the methods, but to know and describe their performance (Wright, 2010).

Intentionally creating methods, seeking out new techniques, and integrating technology to encourage reflection can be ways of improving the outcomes of a process. In developing our own processes, it would help to see not only who, but how others bring reflection and action together. As we assess what we learn from others, it would also help to remember opposites must be balanced in strength and capabilities just as the wings of a bird are to successfully enable flight.

AND NOW FOR SOMETHING COMPLETELY DIFFERENT

It may be easy to look at education to see how reflection and action can be placed together, but we may have a hard time seeing how this applies to any profession. To explore this, let's consider how reflection and action could even be useful in comedy, specifically improv.

In October 2001, the American improvisational comedy show *Whose Line Is It Anyway?* hosted by Drew Carey aired episode 408. In this show, the regular stars Ryan Stiles, Colin Mochrie, and Wayne Brady were joined by guest comic Kathryn Greenwood (Rotten Tomatoes, 2021). About five minutes into the show, Carey introduced the game "Living Scenery" where two performers enacted a scene using the other two performers as props (Fandom, 2021).

For this episode, Stiles and Mochrie acted out a scene of their morning routine and Brady and Greenwood stood in as various props.

> *Stiles and Mochrie laid down onstage and Brady laid*
> *between with his arms draped over them as a blanket.*
> *Mochrie yawned, got up, and cheerfully said, "Good*

morning!" Stiles groaned, "Oh, I didn't hear the alarm go off." Brady started beeping and Mochrie hit him on the head. He then turned toward Greenwood to take a quick shower. She flailed her arms about and made sound effects like water spraying around him. After the shower, Mochrie pulled Brady's outstretched arms back and forth around him to dry off his backside, then placed Brady on a rack.

Mochrie put on Greenwood as a shirt and asked what Stiles thinks. Stiles suggested looking in the mirror, pushing Brady toward Mochrie. Brady moved to mimic Mochrie but added a gesture at his forehead and said "bing" to suggest light was shining brightly off Mochrie's bald head. Mochrie paused, scrunched up his face, and finally said, "There's something wrong with this mirror." Stiles asked, "Would you like waffles this morning?" as he moved Greenwood to the toaster. Mochrie moved Brady beside her. The two squatted and then popped up. Mochrie looked at Brady, an African American, and let out a disappointed, "Oh…" He then pivoted as he moved Brady to his plate, declaring, "Yum! Just the way I like it!" Brady could not contain his laughter (dailymotion, 2021).

If you watch the show faithfully, you can see the cast is able to pull off hilarious moments and week after week, it is hard to imagine the scenes are not scripted or rehearsed. The cast has always said it is truly unscripted and made the show even funnier (Bernardini, 2019). In a 2015 interview with TheCelebrityCafe.com, Mochrie compared improv to a sitcom. In the case of a sitcom, the audience can be taught when to expect a joke, but in improv, no one has an idea when the punchline is going to come, because no one knows how it is being set up. This bit of the unexpected is what makes improv exciting.

The excitement of the unexpected is shown through rigorous studies to improve overall wellbeing. It turns out the spontaneity reduces stress and increases creativity, self-esteem, and motivation. These studies have prompted more than one workplace coaching firm to use improv as a team building exercise in the workplace (Cole, 2016).

So, how does improv work? In a 2021 interview with Mochrie, Kevin Durham asked what his process of improv was and how they were able to create such comedy. Mochrie responded,

"The thing about improv is you have to do everything you're not used to doing in real life. The two basic rules are listening and accepting people's offers…[We are] relaxed enough with each other to actually go out with absolutely nothing and trust it's somehow going to work out. And it's basically just us riffing with each other, listening, accepting, and then building and taking it into whatever direction we decided to go" (Kevin Durham, 2021).

Even something as chaotic as improvisational comedy has a process. In listening to Mochrie, the process involves elements of reflection, such as listening and accepting, and elements of action, namely building and taking it in a direction. To be able to do this, the performers have to trust the other will hear them and respond with something each can use—almost like a friendly game of catch. The two want to contribute to the process and even surprise one another, but not compete with the other, because the trust would be lost.

Take a look back at the scene above on how Mochrie and Brady achieved this.

Stiles and Mochrie laid down and Brady was at the ready as a blanket. Mochrie decided to get up, but Stiles was waiting for the alarm. Brady stepped in making the alarm sound even though he was a blanket. Mochrie went with it and interacted with Brady as one would an alarm clock. To dry off after the shower, Mochrie pushed Brady to interact closely with his backside. When Brady became the mirror, he paid him back by emphasizing Mochrie's shiny head, which was a constant source of teasing in the show. Mochrie paused to create tension in the scene the audience would laugh to release. Stiles moved the scene to creating waffles. No one anticipated the idea Mochrie's waffle was burnt until Brady popped up. Mochrie had many options and he chose the most positive that built trust between them—just the way I like it.

We can learn from Mochrie and Brady as we develop and use our own processes that include reflection and action. They give us a number of options on how to accomplish this. We can see reflection-for-action as Brady chooses to use a running joke of the balding head and reflection-in-action when Mochrie pivots to love the burnt waffle. We can suppose there is reflection-on-action when the entire cast reviews the footage after filming to gauge how the audience reacted so they know what tricks were effective.

While our situation may not be improv, our days can be filled with listening, accepting, and trusting. As we develop our processes, we need to realize using elements of both reflection and action prepare us to listen, and to accept what is offered. When we apply our process, we need to trust everything will work out if we do not try to control the outcome. It is in these moments we can experience what it means to effortlessly glide on our wings of reflection and action and soar to where we aim to go.

INTENTIONALLY CREATING TIMES FOR REFLECTION AND TIMES FOR ACTION

I wanted to dig further into these ideas of how to combine reflection and action and looked for analogies or metaphors. My thought was reflection and action are considered opposites, and I wondered where else people were holding two opposites in their lives. We all have this. We can be mothers and daughters at the same time, or students and teachers. I looked for more unusual pairings, such as engineers who had become designers or foreign nationals from traditionally eastern countries living in the West—people who I knew were likely holding a tension between these two things and had found a way to work with them both.

My first interview was with Hongyang, who had just completed her PhD in design and was working as a design researcher in Arizona. Hongyang was the daughter of two architects and had grown up in Beijing. I asked her how it was to combine the two worlds of her heritage and the US.

"I haven't been wanting to combine. I wouldn't try to just mix them together like a Frankenstein thing. I would say I carry them both at the same time, but sometimes I would like to emphasize one. It could just be in conflict for me. I could gather and create a new thing, I guess, [but] I'm comfortable with those conflicts already. I'm comfortable dealing with the complex, but one day, [I hope] I can smoothly translate from one conflict to another. I don't really know what that will look like, but it might look cool."

I readily thought of a student I had mentored in the College of Design. Mohit was a mechanical engineer from the University of Mumbai who had been introduced to me while working on his Master's in Industrial Design. He had been interested in sustainability and my career was in materials at the time. We readily found we were kindred spirits since we both had started in engineering and then switched to industrial design. We had often traded stories of how our engineering and design sides would fight one another. He had graduated in 2019 and since moved to Austin, Texas, to be the first industrial designer at a provider of custom laboratory furniture and industrial workbenches. I enjoyed the opportunity to catch up and hear how the internal battle was going as he worked in this all-engineering company.

"I have to be open enough to where the project is to be a designer in this engineering company. I have to consciously make an effort to switch off and switch on that [mechanical engineering] side when needed because there are phases in a project where you want to have a bird's eye view and there are phases when you need to have a worm's view. When I look at it from the bird's point of view, the designer side of me was helpful, but when I wanted to look at it from the worm's point of view, I thought the more detail-oriented side I had from engineering was helpful. Being able to switch helps me communicate with a bunch of engineers who have not seen the design process and do not understand what I bring to the project."

Hongyang recognized she was carrying a Chinese side and an American side and perceived these sat in conflict. She decided to emphasize her Chinese side or her American side depending on the situation but has never brought both out at the same time. Mohit carried the role of a designer into an organization that was filled with engineers. Having been an engineer, he understood his coworkers well. He then cherry-picked the strengths of the designer and the engineer within him and applied either when the situation called for that talent. While he did carry both together, he also did not bring them both out at the same time.

It then seemed that action and reflection could coexist, but would only be brought out separately when needed, depending on the task or audience. I can imagine researchers would see this as reflection-for-action where Hongyang and Mohit are looking ahead at the situation and choose which opposite to bring out. There likely are times when they look back at how things went in the situation, and researchers would call this reflection-on-action.

To me, then, reflection or action could be viewed as tools in a toolbox that can be brought into a process as needed. That sat well with me and I felt others would appreciate that, so I kept asking others I interviewed the same question. Can reflection and action coexist?

REFLECTING AS I ACT

I started to accumulate other examples of how people utilized separate times of reflection and action within their processes. I wanted to find someone who could explain how to use reflection and action at the same time. I finally found Stacy Levy.

Stacy Levy is a sculptor who works with the natural patterns of nature within an urban environment. She began her career in urban forestry with more constraints than she preferred and found becoming an environmental artist more freeing. I asked her how much she dealt with the idea of gut versus head and reflection versus action in her design process.

> *"I've never separated the reflection versus the action, because I am performing the action and reflecting very simultaneously. It's rare there's action without reflection going on at the same time. Your right hand is reaching to stick something in there. Your left hand is going, 'Hmmm, is that...maybe?' So, unless we've vetted*

everything and...there's sort of nothing else materials can do except fit into these places, I think there's always reflection that goes on."

Simultaneously? I dug further to see if this happens more often than I realized. I had not noticed because those who do it switch back and forth so quickly we cannot see it. It literally happens in the moment. How many times has a teacher changed the lesson for the day based on a question from the class? Or an ER nurse completely changed treatment based on how the patient responded? Or a writer took the story in a different tangent due to a new muse? Or the design of a product changed during the sketches in ideation?

Levy describes this as, "'It's like you're pushing a ball. You're not gripping the thing, but you're pushing it and it's rolling in places and you're guiding it, but it may go somewhere you didn't expect and you continue to guide it. But you listen to what this big sphere moving through your piece is saying, which is, 'This doesn't work or this is better when it's like this,' and you try and do as much change as you can to the piece."

To some, this may sound far too chaotic. Levy gives a reason to try.

"You have to always leave room for changing your direction. You start setting something up [and see] 'This really doesn't look that good. We got to change this.' If you are nervous about the outcome, then you are likely in the right place. I have to be open for that. I think that what artists bring to the table is a) we're much more

risk-taking and b) we're much more into the idea there
is a better idea that could be embraced midway in the
process. Possibility comes with risk."

There is comfort in a repeatable process that lets us assume the outcome is repeatable—like baking a cake. The truth is the outcome is dependent on so many variables that are out of our control. When I take Levy's advice, I encourage myself as I plan to make space for where the process may take a right turn and to also become open to the potential of how beautiful the unplanned outcome may be. If I let this be my mindset, I then am able to receive so much more.

BELIEVING IN SOMETHING BETTER

Whether we choose to follow Hongyang and Mohit with keeping these opposites apart or Stacy with using reflection and action simultaneously, the crucial point is a healthy process will use reflection and action to support each other in various ways. We can see how this worked for Mochrie and Brady in their improv. From the Introduction, we can also see how Messi instinctually made sure his actions were from reflecting on the situation on the soccer field. Similarly, from Chapter Two, we can see how Yo-Yo Ma intentionally set up his cello practice to be more successful and efficient by spending time to research his desire for a piece of music.

When we can set up processes that intentionally have elements of reflection and action, we take Levy's advice and "leave room for changing direction." Mochrie and Brady, Messi, and Ma all believe something better could reveal itself in the middle of the action. The only difference in the application is how or when one chooses to pay attention to what is revealed. If we are a beginner, then it may be we need to spend time looking back at what happened to see the new opportunity. If we are more advanced, we could look ahead and plan for different scenarios that could play out while we act. The elite, though, have enough skills and practice that they have the space within their minds to process the information immediately so they can change their actions in the moment. The key when applying our chosen method is to believe there could be something better in the middle of our process, then we are more apt to listen and accept what is offered in reflection and take the risk to find our potential.

Ultimately, the methods and application of reflection and action for our process is our choice. The beauty of including reflective elements is having the chance to understand the quality of those choices, and then we will better know what actions to take. With both of these elements secure in our process, we can then understand what it means to have two wings instead of one supporting us as we fly.

FOUR

Developing Your
Own Process

———

"It's better to be a pirate than to join the Navy."

— STEVE JOBS (TODD, 2019)

In 1983, Apple was developing the first Mac and some employees were losing faith. At an offsite retreat, Jobs sought to motivate with this adage reminding them as pirates, they were free from bureaucracy and able to take more risks in order to strive for greater rewards (Todd, 2019).

His assertion is understandable. Consider how difficult decision-making can be within the bureaucracy of the US Navy, which resides within the more complex US Department of Defense that is also housed within the US government, the largest bureaucracy in the world (Montgomery, 2017).

While there can be good reasons for creating a bureaucratic government, the rules enacted by bureaucracies can be taken too far and leaders may be so indoctrinated they cannot see outside of the overwhelming maze (Sparknotes, 2021; Montgomery, 2017). The result can be the inability for the organization to respond when needed. For example, since 2001, the number and changes in military situations around the world have caused such an increase in US missions that the decision-making process has ground to a halt. The results have been distressing for employees when purchasing the needed technology for new missions. To become more agile and to adapt to a changing world stage, technologies, and evolving societies, the Department of Defense has made cutting red tape a priority, declaring, to be successful, this will be a never-ending, diligent effort (Roulo, 2014).

Is it any wonder then that Jobs wanted his team to be pirates freed from the bureaucracy of the rules and structures within Apple?

It makes me ponder: Is it true the only way to make something new successful is to completely leave the existing system? If you develop your own process, must you leave all you have known before?

Is it truly better to become a pirate?

IT DEPENDS

I believe the answer is, "It depends." We all are unique and perform differently than anyone else. A cookie cutter process cannot work for everyone and every situation. We can look to known processes and even principles for guidance, but it is always best to intentionally choose those elements that enhance our lives versus blindly following them in a herd mentality. Choosing to create our own process, whether it is completely unique or blends with tried-and- true methods, allows us to maximize what we are able to do. To do this, each of us must reflect on who we are, what we want to achieve, and how we work best. Becoming that best version of ourselves is the highest work we can achieve.

I bet Captain Chesley Sullenberger would agree. On January 15, 2009, he was piloting US Airways Flight 1549 as it took off from LaGuardia Airport en route to Charlotte. Within the first one hundred seconds, a flock of geese collided with the plane, disabling both engines. Captain "Sully" Sullenberger, with forty-two years of Air Force and commercial flying experience, knew this flight would be like nothing he had ever trained for (Inc., 2009).

Without a word between them, the first officer, Jeff Skiles, took over the checklist for the engine restart and the captain took control of the plane (Inc., 2009; National Transportation Safety Board, 2021). Sully knew the checklist well enough to see ahead and took two remedial actions that would be handled too late if he only stuck to the checklist. He turned on the engine ignition and the airplane's auxiliary power. He needed those actions to be effective immediately so he could focus on how he would influence the way this plane would intersect with the earth a few minutes later.

The plane was over New York City. Two airport runways at two different airports were made available, but Sully knew they could not make it to either airport. The last option, in the most developed metro area in the world, was the Hudson River.

Sully made his choice.

The airplane was descending like an elevator at two floors per second. The last critical step for Sully was to raise the nose of the airplane to slow the descent and get in the best possible position before the plane hit the river. The water was missing all the features a pilot would have on an airport runway, so the ability to judge when and how to land the plane was difficult. Again wordlessly, the two pilots worked together. Jeff Skiles started calling out airspeed and altitude so Sully could focus on the water and the horizon.

About five minutes after taking off, the plane landed hard and some were seriously injured, but all 155 passengers and crew survived the landing. By the time Sully left the plane after everyone else had already escaped to the wings, the New York waterway ferries had arrived to move everyone to safety (Inc., 2009).

The situation was unique and certainly not anticipated by any process, regulation, or procedure. Yet as you can see, Captain Sullenberger pulled from his forty-two years of experience, assessed what was useful, and moved creatively to the solution. He and Jeff Skiles adapted to each step in the situation by using existing procedures and creating new processes as needed.

This developing process was not something that just happened in those five minutes or even that day. At the 2010 National Press Club Author's Night, Sully said to write his memoir *Highest Duty,* he "had to have an insightful survey of my life [and] all the important events and the people who were with me that day. [It all] helped me synthesize a lifetime of experiences to solve a problem I'd never seen before, along with my crew" (Sullenberger, 2009; C-Span, 2010).

BRINGING OUT YOUR BEST

We can understand how Sully can be a hero when breaking the rules to manage a life-threatening situation. However, since few of us will ever be in that situation, are we justified in breaking rules or not going along with the system in place? Does it matter if those of us in mundane situations become pirates?

Harvard behavioral scientist Francesca Gino would say it is better for all of us if there are some who break the rules. She was so inspired by her research she wrote the book *Rebel Talent.* She hoped her findings would shift the thinking about rebels as arrogant troublemakers to people who break rules in constructive and productive ways that are positive for their lives, families, and organizations.

Her research of rebels led her to five common characteristics. Rebels go against the status quo and do what it takes to solve the problem; they jump in to help even if it makes them look weak; they are okay with feeling uncomfortable; they play to their strengths and enable others to do the same; and they see accidents as a source of inspiration.

In 2011, she applied her research theories to a company called Wipro Technologies in India. Wipro is a call center that had a 70 percent turnover rate of their employees within their first sixty days. She created a modified onboarding process and compared one group of new hires in the modified process to another group in the original process. She simply gave those in the modified process group a half hour of reflection to consider their unique qualities, their strengths, and how they felt they could play to those strengths at work.

Seven months later, she interviewed those in the study still with Wipro. She found the reflectors, or those given the time to reflect, were almost 20 percent more likely to still be at Wipro and received higher ratings in their customers' calls. She concluded those moments of reflection made the new hires feel more authentic, and it turns out authenticity brings out those five rebel characteristics.

She found this interesting considering the positions in this call center were very rigid, which suggests her findings were true no matter what industry or job someone had. The key, she writes, is "when we challenge ourselves to move beyond what we know and can do well, we rebel against the comfortable cocoon of the status quo, improving ourselves and positioning ourselves to contribute more to our partners, coworkers, and organizations" (Gino, 2018; Talks at Google, 2018).

Being rebel talent is making sure you are being an authentic extension of your best self in whatever you are called to do. No matter how wide open or bureaucratic the system, or how flamboyant or conservative you are, being your best self is actually the highest calling there is. With that definition, you could actually be a pirate *in* the Navy.

GIVING YOURSELF PERMISSION

While I appreciate the confines of a call center job, I find it interesting Gino does not emphasize cultural norms. I wondered if her use of reflection in the onboarding process may have given these employees permission to not only rebel against the corporate status quo, but against societal pressures. Whether it be East versus West, or millennials versus baby boomers, there are differences in cultures that influence what we think, how we feel, and ultimately how we act. Reflection can give us a moment to consider those differences so we can give ourselves permission to choose what is the best for us.

In 2012, researchers from Columbia Business School and the Ramaiah Institute of Technology tested the claim Indians are more likely than Americans to defer to authority figures. They conducted numerous studies to understand if that was true, as well as diving into the motivations that made one defer. They explored these issues by looking at how female participants responded to another's opinion on whether or not they should wear sleeveless clothing for a New Year's Eve party. The study proved Indian participants were more likely to wear the clothing their father preferred while Americans would not be swayed.

They also studied how a boss's opinion on professional development courses influenced their employees. The Indian participants chose job-relevant courses assuming the boss would approve, but the study also found when evaluating the courses, the Indians would share their own opinion versus mimicking their boss's. Alternatively, Americans would take whatever course they wanted despite their boss's preference, but if they knew their boss's opinion of the quality of the course, they would be more likely to share a less favorable opinion in the evaluation as a way of rebelling (Savani, 2011).

Rebelling can be difficult when the cultural norms call for deference to an authority figure. Sometimes the only way to let your voice be heard is to step away from the culture, the country, and the system. In that case, one can feel like a pirate.

I learned this from Dnyanada.

An Indian living in the United States, Dnyanada has opened up to a number of choices on how to live her life. She says, though, her choices are not about deference or rebellion.

"There are certain things that probably come naturally to you and it's just in your nature. You can't just separate out [the differences in culture]."

Still, she struggles with the differences in her traditional upbringing and the norms of the US culture. While she was in college, Dnyanada was shocked her friends would challenge their parents. Now that she is married with a child, she and her Indian husband have chosen to share the household chores more than their parents might have.

When I asked if there were any changes she would prefer to make in her career, she admitted she would like to be more action-oriented, similar to those in Western cultures, because "it is not something that comes naturally. It's an acquired skill…and it takes a lot more energy." She told me of a time when she went to her mentor with an issue she was struggling with. As she waited for the solution to be handed to her on a platter, the mentor asked, "What do you think about it?" While Dnyanada had her own thoughts about the situation, she didn't know she was supposed to be ready with an answer.

She now knows to be ready to give her opinion as part of the discussion. She actively engages with the other people to create something better together. She found this in a special training her employer had organized where she worked with a coach and a small group of women on specific topics of their own choosing. With this support group, she learned how to give herself permission to step out into this new space and lead not only herself, but others, like her brand-new daughter.

Dnyanada is a perfect example of one who has not abandoned her upbringing or years of experience. In those years, her parents had given her tools to be able to make wise choices, and she still relies on them. The key is she has embraced the freedom to reflect on what she wants her life to be. She has created a blending of the old and new to make the best life for herself, her employer, and her family.

ORBITING THE GIANT HAIRBALL (MACKENZIE, 1998)

My time with Dnyanada inspired me to find my way of doing things. As with everything that is new, there come moments that feel full of despair. I recalled one such time in writing my first chapter for my first book.

I had finished my first attempt at a book chapter earlier in the week. It wasn't perfect, but I felt it was something of value. My editor liked the content and pointed out there were better places to use it. There were options on what to do and I wasn't sure where to even begin. I had not been through the lecture on chapter writing. It's typical of me to try something out before I have the instructions. How many times had I built ready-to-assemble furniture with the instructions cast aside, only to get stuck and go hunting through the trash for them? I snickered a bit and sighed. I always make my own stress.

The lecture was straightforward with templates, directions, and examples of what to do. The professor was attempting to make this as easy as possible. He was showing us secret tips and tricks on how to write a book. That was why I was in this class.

Yet with each passing slide, I became more unnerved. Templates created simplicity where previously written content could be plugged in, gaps would need to be filled, and the overall text would be polished into a mediocre draft. This was my first issue. While I had fifteen thousand words, I did not have Lego blocks to plug into templates. Maybe because my words were in large chunks with little variety; maybe because there were too many themes to explore; maybe because I needed more structure on what I wanted to say. In any case, I was starting with a blank sheet of paper.

I felt the pressure of a deadline and knew I needed to get to work filling the pages up. The lectures presented structures to place on these blank sheets to make this a bit like paint-by-numbers art. I saw the beauty in the process, but the image the paint-by-numbers created was not resonating with me. There didn't seem to be time to figure that out on my own, so that voice inside pushed me to conform to the process.

Somewhere deep inside, something starting shouting, *"No!"* I can only conform to so many rules at once and this year had already been piling them on: stick to your process, wear a mask, wash your hands, keep six feet away, don't go out, cook for yourself, decorate for Christmas, buy everyone a gift, mail all those gifts, send out Christmas greetings, write five hundred words a day, look for a job, update your resume, make a portfolio, get that interview, keep making calls, and whatever you do, don't ever stop...

Conforming to this template put me over my rule limit. I shut down.

I sat in front of my Mac with my head in my hands, fighting the tears that were demanding to come. I must have uttered the *"No!"* out loud because my dear black Labrador, Lucy, was then wiggling around my legs, banging her tail against the table. I looked down at this fit of joy and stroked her head. Whatever would I do without her? Lucy was right. I needed a break.

A couple days later, I was sitting in the chair where I began my day reflecting on wherever my mind went. The book *Orbiting the Giant Hairball* by Gordon MacKenzie floated in. MacKenzie was a creative at Hallmark and found in corporations, creatives thrive best if they are able to be themselves. The collective creates a hairball of rules needed to make a functioning business survive. Creatives need to be outside of the hairball but connected in an orbit. If they are pulled into the collective, the sheer gravity of having to conform will stifle all the creative genius out of them. They will suffocate in the hairball (MacKenzie, 1998).

As I was going through the lecture, something inside of me was rebelling to survive. Being reminded of the hairball and my need to creatively breathe helped me consider how to orbit the templates. I pulled them out and examined each section individually. What does this mean to the professor and editor? What part resonates with me? How can I create a simpler version that creates structure and allows for breathing room?

I can look to their expertise, but ultimately to create something authentic, I need to make it my own for something this important to me. Giving myself permission to be my authentic self freed me to then accept the help that was being offered and create the best I could create.

YOUR MISSION SHOULD YOU CHOOSE TO ACCEPT IT

Developing your own process is no easy task. It can seem overwhelming when sitting from a place of burnout. Still, it is worth it to reengage with the world. Your authentic self is what you and this world need.

Developing your own process is the best way to bring out your best self so you can offer your unique gift. Give yourself permission to go places you have never been before. Reflect on the core knowledge that allows you to pull from years of experience. Take the time to listen to that inner wisdom on what needs to be kept and what needs to be made anew.

There are no rules and no one right answer. Your process may have aspects that look like mine or something else entirely. Although there is definitely one wrong answer—not making this your own. Without ensuring you are being authentic, the result will not be the same.

Gordon MacKenzie says it well:

"You have a masterpiece inside you, you know. One unlike any that has ever been created, or ever will be. If you go to your grave without painting your masterpiece, it will not get painted. No one else can paint it. Only you" (MacKenzie, 1998).

PART TWO

PRINCIPLES

FIVE

Shift the Mindset

———

""Everyday Is a Winding Road" started out as kind of a road song, and it really wound up being about being in the moment and not always looking to the next moment and analyzing things. As I look at this record, stepping away from it, I realize thematically a lot of it is about...finding levity in life...and trying to figure out how to make all things work simultane-ously without grand disruption. That's kind of what the song is about. It's about jumping in a truck with a guy who just lives life every minute, by the minute. Every once in a while, I have to catch myself and remind myself that life is right now. It's not two minutes from now."

— SHERYL CROW (SONGFACTS, 2021)

To many of her fans, it would come as a surprise Sheryl Crow started her career with stage fright. "The biggest part of my early career, I just didn't want to see the audience at all," said Crow. "I became like a shoegazer" (Larratt, 2020). It is a surprise because Crow's debut album was a huge success. It sold more than seven million copies in the US and the UK that year and won her three Grammy Awards for Record of the Year, Best New Artist, and Best Female Vocal Performance (Huey, 2021). Despite the stage fright, she continued and has navigated a thirty-year music career, produced eleven albums, sold over fifty million of them, and won nine Grammys (Kelly et. al., 2019).

At the age of forty-four, something happened that gave her a new perspective. Crow was diagnosed with breast cancer. No family history or risk factors warned her. Fortunately, early detection resulted in successful treatments to becoming cancer-free (National Breast Cancer Foundation, 2021).

Still, even when emerging as a survivor, having to face one's own mortality is a life-changing experience that causes most to see life differently. From then on, Crow was able to see a larger picture of what was going on when she was on stage and to readily look up at her audience.

"There was a moment where I realized what we do isn't necessarily all about us: it's about the eye contact, it's about the electricity or whatever it is in the room that moves perfect strangers. That is what music does," said Crow (Larratt, 2020).

Just as Crow found a new perspective that moved her from fear of connecting with her audience, we have the opportunity to live a life that moves us and those around us by being open to shifting our mindset. We can see from Crow's story that fear, particularly fear of failure, can encourage us to make everything about us and miss those moments when we can look up and connect with someone or something outside of ourselves. Fear is not the only thing that could hold us hostage. There are other intense things like anger, hostility, or resentment, but there can be softer things such as apathy, habits, or biases.

Positive or negative, strong or weak, there is something keeping our minds engaged with the system that promotes constant action that leads to burnout. To break free, we will need to examine what our preconceived notions are, decide what needs to be changed, and make the shift to a new way of thinking. With that shift in thinking, we allow ourselves to design a new process instead of simply recreating everything we have always done. We give ourselves the chance to connect to something outside of us and plug into the electricity that makes us want to engage with what we are doing.

WHAT IS A SHIFT IN MINDSET?

A paradigm shift can be defined as "a major change in the concepts and practices of how something works or is accomplished" (Kenton, 2019). A good example is the Industrial Revolution, where the focus of society moved from a farming, rural-based community to a factory-based, urban community. For better or for worse, this paradigm shift ultimately created capitalism, a middle class, and modern cities (Chen, 2021).

A paradigm is the way we perceive reality. A shift in a paradigm can require a change in how one thinks about our experience, what someone does in the new reality, and how things are made in the future. A paradigm shift requires considering trade-offs. For example, moving off the farm meant children would no longer grow up there and inherently learn where food comes from, how life begins and ends, and what happens in each season.

A common perception of reality today is constant action is what is necessary to succeed. To shift our reality to one that includes reflection with our actions, we need to understand what we are giving up, what we can gain today and in the future, and consciously make the choice to shift. In other words, we first need to shift our mindset to see the benefits of developing our own process so we will be motivated to put in the work that is needed to make our process a reality.

OUTGROWING WHERE YOU ARE

It is easy to understand shifting one's mindset when you are facing cancer as Sheryl Crow did. If we were to seek out such benefits to shifting, are there ways for us to catalyze the shift without having to face life-threatening situations? I posed this question to my LinkedIn followers and many mentioned one big shift was when they moved away from home to go to college. In general, it was the shift from living in the family unit to being responsible for everything yourself. It is a big shift that grows bigger as one graduates and moves into the workforce.

Spending one summer back at home while I was in college, I remember well when I came face to face with how much I had changed. Are any of us prepared for how we feel when we return home after such big shifts? Dr. Engin Kapkin, at Eskişehir Technical University in Turkey, weighed in with his thoughts when I posed the question to him.

Engin is an industrial designer who researches how people generate and attribute meaning in their lives, particularly when it comes to their interaction with products or places. He wants to understand how people add meaning to the things around them. He has looked closely over the years and found there are multiple levels to meaning. What is most interesting to him is there is a microlevel of very tiny things happening every day that either validate our definition of meaning or add something new to it. He gave an example.

> *Say you look about your room and decide you need a chair right over there by the window. You go shopping for a chair, buy one, bring it home, and put in your room. You spend decades enjoying that chair in that spot. One day, your neighbor's cat slips through your door and decides to make a litter box out of your chair. There is no cleaning that will ever remove the smell. To let the chair go feels like someone died. There are too many microlevel memories associated that give meaning to that chair.*

The same thing happens in connection to where one is from. Engin is a Turkish man living in Turkey and is part of the neighborhood, culture, and nation. That top-level definition affects everything he thinks and does in ways that are not noticeable. It took living in the US for many years before he began to realize the effect his culture had on his choices.

The first year living abroad was perfect, everything was new and exciting. However, the second year was difficult when he allowed the new culture to touch him. Instead of sitting on the outside, he decided to find a girlfriend. He is a funny guy who enjoys a good joke and luckily found a girl who also liked to laugh. The problem was he didn't get her jokes and was not sure what was wrong. Reflecting, he realized her jokes were connected to a memory in her childhood, like a cartoon she loved to watch, and he did not share that experience. He felt the weight of the difference between them. He wondered if he could ever permanently work in the US and make friends if he could not make people smile.

In the struggle, Engin looked back at life in Turkey. He empathized more with how people lived because he understood better the reasoning behind the choices people made. He began to know more about his people and even more about himself. The observations and reflections also helped him know more about the American people. He could open up to seeing similarities—such as both nations being made of immigrants and people always asking one another, "Where are you from?" This time of reflection transformed him into an observer of everything about himself and not just part of either culture.

The Turkish have a word for this: "gurbet." It can simply mean to live abroad in a foreign country and longing for your homeland. It can also be that "state or feeling of being a stranger" (Wiktionary, 2021). Engin says this is more than homesickness. Gurbet begins when you move back home to your country and realize life went on without you. The things you longed for while you were away are not the same.

He also realized his life went on without them. He had new habits that were different from those common in the Turkish culture. He found while he was in the US using a calendar and being prompt to meetings was valued, so he adopted the custom. When he returned to Turkey, he had forgotten setting meetings on a calendar was generally not done and continued his habit of promptly showing up for a meeting. As he sat in an empty conference room waiting for people to arrive, he knew the connection was lost and he didn't belong there anymore. Much like trying to let go of the chair, he felt like someone had died.

Moving past the grief of loss, Engin dug deeper and saw who he was outside all of his experiences. In other words, he knew what he was capable of so well that when these feelings of not belonging cropped up, it was not a problem. He knew it was not about the culture or understanding someone's jokes. His life was about himself, what he liked to do, who he wanted to spend time with, and where he wanted to live. And that was it. He had come to realize he didn't belong anywhere. He was grateful to have a backpack of experiences and knowledge to let him travel wherever he wanted to go. "I feel more confident I can make whatever I want. I feel powerful because I have the control over things in my life I never used to have before."

He then belonged to himself.

Engin's story shows us two new ways of thinking. First, change is always happening, particularly the way we think, even when we do not notice. Our reality is made up of a million microscopic experiences, thoughts, and interactions we have and will accumulate. Secondly, we can catalyze our shift in mindset, without facing life-threatening situations, by embracing change through seeking out new experiences foreign to what we have always known. Initially, the catalyst will start as an exciting adventure, but we need to give those experiences long enough to touch us to allow for a true paradigm shift. In the short term, this can be uncomfortable, but the shift will increase our long-term joy and peace.

OBSERVING AMBIGUITY

Paradigm shifts can be hard and require enormous amounts of time and energy. The entire experience can be exhilarating and disorienting. Just when we think we have everything figured out, our entire world can change. We are thrown off balance and life can feel as if it is spinning out of our control.

I was not looking for an opportunity to develop my own process. On the contrary, I was looking for a job and the global pandemic of 2020 took over my daily life as it did so many others. I was readily seeing I would need to be open to other options on how I would survive. I generally enjoy ambiguity because I see it as a puzzle that needs to be solved. The true definition of ambiguity is "the quality of being open to more than one interpretation" (Google Dictionary, 2021). Being faced with more than one solution did make my world spin. Not because I didn't enjoy the idea of having options; it was more I found comfort in making decisions, and I was in a place with too many options. There was a voice that kept nagging me to figure that out, but I was struggling to find the puzzle pieces.

I chose to develop a reflective process as a way to manage my life and help me relieve this nagging. The process would help me understand my options: Should I look for a job I was overqualified for? Should I start my own business? Should I become a working artist? Should I change careers again and start teaching? The process would also help me understand how to differentiate myself. What did I have to offer? What was I best at? What decisions could I make quickly and what needed to marinate for a while?

When my mind is approaching something new with so many options, I prefer to anchor myself in something tangible and often look to nature for what is similar in the hopes of finding a metaphor that leads to a solution. In this case, I found vertigo. Different than a fear of heights, vertigo is the sensation of feeling off-balance, or even as extreme as the world around you spinning. Problems in the inner ear, such as an infection, changes in pressure, or dislodged particles, can cause vertigo.

The inner ear collects information it sends to the brain through the vestibular system so the brain can in turn send out information to the head and body on what adjustments to make relative to gravity. When that information is confused by the problems in the inner ear, the brain interprets the body and head need to be adjusted. At the same time, gravity is pulling in the same direction it always is. This conflict in what is reality can make a person feel a swaying, tilting, spinning, or pulling in one direction. The feeling can be accompanied by nausea, vomiting, headaches, sweating, and jerking eye movements that can last for just a few minutes or even hours.

This information resonated with me, but I wanted more than just information. What could I do about it? Reading further, I found depending on the type of inner ear problem, doctors can lay out a course of treatments, but often there is no treatment suggested because the brain eventually adapts to the new messages it is receiving from the inner ear. In cases the brain does not adjust completely, physical therapy is recommended to help the patient manage the vertigo (Ambardekar, 2020).

One such therapy, called the Epley maneuver, is used for moving dislodged particles back into their correct place within the ear. The patient starts by sitting on the edge of the bed. A pillow is on the bed behind them. The patient tilts their head to the side and quickly lays back with their head hanging off the pillow. After a minute, the head is tilted over the other shoulder. After another minute, the patient rolls over onto the shoulder to lower the head further.

Gravity moves the particles through the circular tubes in the inner ear much like how tilting a wooden maze game moves a metal ball to the center of the puzzle. Once the particles are back where they belong, the vertigo will cease for some time, if not forever (Fauquier ENT, 2014). Studies have shown for 72 percent of people with the dislodged particle vertigo, one session of the Epley maneuver is all it takes to eliminate the vertigo, and 90 percent found relief after repeating it a few times over the following week (Gaur, 2015).

This for me is a good metaphor for what to do when I am going through a paradigm shift. When I am experiencing the overwhelming spinning, it is good to realize a number of factors are pulling at me and the information I am receiving may be confusing me to act when I should not. I need to remain open to the fact there is more than one interpretation to what is happening.

In these times, it is good for me to find a safe place to lay back, let the particles of information settle, and observe how my vision comes back into focus. The clarity gives me a chance to learn something in those moments of ambiguity.

As I learn, I have a better chance to make choices that are meaningful to me in the long term. I can use the clarity to see what kind of process will serve me best. I can also see what action I need to take to eliminate what is not serving me well. Whatever choices are made, I can be confident my choices are freeing me from where I am and will take me somewhere new. That knowledge always gives me great hope that what I work on will lead to success.

LEANING INTO TENSION

Being overwhelmed to the point of spinning can definitely cause stress and tension, but as we can see, there can also be moments of opportunity. Faced with the choice, it may seem right to avoid the tension, but with enough experience, we can realize in order to capture the opportunity, we need to be curious about the tension, engage with it, and even lean into it.

If we continue with the vertigo metaphor, we could be going through a shift in mindset; we feel the world is spinning and we act to gain some clarity on how to move forward. Once things are clear, we can see there may be multiple factors that influence the details of our choices. Some of the factors can be in opposition to each other, and on first glance, it may seem we can only choose between one or the other, such as the first time someone considers when to use reflection and action. It may first seem like these are separate and distinct factors to a process that cannot be put together, but we have seen from Chapter Three it is possible to have both in the same process and even in the same moment.

The tension we feel when thinking of combining opposites, such as reflection and action, can emerge similar to a flashing light. It is not necessarily warning us off but encouraging us to dig deeper into what is happening. We have a chance to learn what is behind the tension, and that knowledge could teach us how to create something completely different. Having opposites together teaches us new insights that could not be achieved with only one of the factors.

The paradigm shift of the Internet has been a source of tension for many industries that traditionally have been tied to physical retail stores. The music industry is a prime example with consumers moving away from record stores to online sourcing of music, and Sheryl Crow had watched all the changes in her three-decade career. Crow was successful and likely had enough money to live comfortably. She could have simply walked away from her music career, but she chose to engage with her passion of music and looked more closely at the tension the online trends were making. She chose to embrace this as an opportunity to find a new method of getting music to her fans.

In 2019, Sheryl Crow released *Threads*, her final full-length album, where she collaborated with a number of the artists who have inspired her career (Kelly et. al., 2019). She also chose to work with some of the younger artists to encourage them to continue inspiring people with their music (Sheryl Crow, 2021). This was her last album not because she was walking away from her career, but she was choosing to move away from albums to releasing only singles because of how the Internet had changed the way people pick and consume music. Listening to an album from beginning to end was a dying art form (Kelly et. al., 2019). She was not fighting the paradigm shift; she was leaning into the tension it created.

There were two types of tension for her with this last album. First, there were the changes in the industry that had caused most musicians to make no money. There were no long-term record deals and to see significant income, extraordinary numbers of online hits were needed. The alternative was live shows where the ticket prices were raised to make up the difference. The visuals of social media were crowding out the actual music, but without them, an artist could not keep the public's short attention span (Clark, 2021).

The second tension for the fifty-seven-year-old Crow was the Pandora's box of microlevel memories from across her career. She told *Entertainment Weekly*, "When I step back from [*Threads*] and listen to it, it's very emotional for me, knowing this is the culmination of not only thirty years, but it goes back to me literally lying under the piano [as a little girl] studying [James Taylor's] *Mud Slide Slim and the Blue Horizon* and [Carole King's] *Tapestry* and all the records that inspired me to do what I'm doing. And all the people who stood up for the things they believed in and made it okay for me to do the same. I'm just filled with gratitude and awe" (Rodman, 2019).

THE NEW NORMAL

Crow's life and music advise us to jump into life right now where it is. I agree in tasting and being present in every moment of life, but I also believe the collection of a million tiny microlevel moments creates meaning to what we are doing. The collective view puts today's moment in perspective so we can enjoy it and allows us to be open to the paradigm shifts that inevitably will come. We can lie back and enjoy the show, knowing if this day isn't our best, there is another opportunity tomorrow—or better yet, if we have had a string of stellar days, the pressure of making today stellar isn't so high, because it is about the accumulation of our days. We can trust with every day, we are a little closer to designing a life we love.

This shift in mindset allows us to develop a process that supports rather than rules us. We can adjust as we change, and we cannot only be present for those beautiful microlevel moments, but even create a space for them to be more of the kind we want.

SIX

Be Inspired by Nature

"I have an interest in biologically inspired discovery, and it has increased over the last ten years. We've learned a great deal from studying nature's anatomical and physiological modifications that allow [the woodpecker] to strike its head so many times and not so much as get a concussion."

— DR. JULIAN BAILES, PORTRAYED BY ALEC BALDWIN
IN THE 2015 FILM *CONCUSSION* (HIMMELL, 2016)

Woodpeckers are omnivores who seek out insects, larvae, eggs, nuts, and even tree sap within a tree trunk. They are able to peck with their chisel-like bill in a cycle up to twenty times per second to drill for their prize (SoftSchools, 2021). That is a speed nearing fifteen miles per hour (Soniak, 2014). In terms of force, that could be resaid as coming to a complete stop when moving at twenty-six thousand miles per hour (Roberts, 2016). The woodpecker will likely repeat this up to twelve thousand times a day. With a lifespan of eleven years in the wild, this bird could bang its head forty-eight million times (SoftSchools, 2021).

Despite all the collisions, the birds are not in pain and are not injured. For anyone who had to take a moment to let the stars fade after hitting their head, it is amazing to consider how the woodpecker keeps going unfazed. For humans, this can be more than just a momentary bit of dizziness. The Center for Disease Control reports between 1.6 and 3.8 million sport- and recreation-related head injuries happen annually, and there is growing concern around the cumulative effect of repeated injuries, particularly in sports like American football (Q30 Innovations, 2021). These injuries have been shown to contribute to problems with memory loss, thinking, depression, and mental health later in life (Boston University, 2021).

What is unique to woodpeckers that makes them so extraordinarily immune to concussions? And if we can understand it, is there some way we can use it to prevent concussions in humans?

In 2007, a physician, Dr. David Smith, was working with members of the military on advanced wound care. The subject of concussions came up and someone casually made a comment the good doctor needed to figure out why woodpeckers readily survive banging their heads.

Dr. Smith heard the offhand comment and started to research not only woodpeckers, but head-ramming sheep and diving birds. He found one thing they all had in common. There is a muscle that compresses their jugular vein during the collision, and the body's response is to increase the amount of blood in the skull. More blood around the brain means it has less room to jostle around and is less likely to then strike the skull from the inside (Viviano, 2017).

Dr. Julian Bales was working as the Chair of Neurosurgery at NorthShore University HealthSystem in Chicago and as a consultant to the NFL. He focused his research interest on the brain and spinal cord with a hope to make a difference in patients' lives (Northshore, 2021). Bailes readily knew helmets could prevent fracturing of the skull, but there was nothing helmets could do about the brain striking inside the skull. He had worked with a number of methods to reduce brain injuries and saw only a 5 percent decrease in trauma. In 2012, Dr. Bailes tested Dr. Smith's theory by fitting a group of rats with a collar to create the compression on the jugular. The results showed an amazing 83 percent reduction in damage to the brain (Turner, 2012).

A startup company, Q30 Innovations, was created and the product development company, Priority Designs, was brought in to take the concept to reality. With a simple, award-winning design of their idea, the researchers have been able to conduct seven pre-clinical trials and sixteen clinical trials—including more than one thousand athletes from three different sports—and collected data from over half a million impacts. The studies have shown significant reduction in changes to the brain when wearing the collar during play. After seven years of development and twenty million dollars in research, Q30 Innovations was able to bring the product to market in Canada in 2017 and through the US FDA approval process in 2020. The company hoped to soon be cleared for market launch in the US to further protect the brain of all athletes (Q30 Innovations, 2021).

When we think of protecting the body, we think of armor and helmets from the Roman times or the Middle Ages. Better designs have been developed since, but they still only protected the head from the outside. Protecting the brain within the skull required a twenty-first century study of the woodpecker. It is often good to look outside of what we know or think we know to be able to find what will help us solve the most wicked of problems. Nature has always been solving complex problems, and it is a great source of inspiration.

While nature can inspire us in product development, it can also teach us about methods. As we look to managing our lives and developing our own processes, we can be faced with chaos, complexity, and trade-offs. Looking to nature can help us navigate this complexity by teaching us the advantages of noticing, defining, and applying the use of patterns we observe. Keeping those advantages in mind can help us trust we have chosen solid methods to adopt.

DEFINING NATURE

When we look to nature, where should we be looking?

According to the Google dictionary, the noun *nature* is primarily defined as "the phenomena of the physical world collectively, including plants, animals, the landscape, and other features and products of the earth, as opposed to humans or human creations" (Google, 2021). When most think of nature, this is likely the definition. We can readily look out the window to see trees, birds, the sun and moon, or the changing of the seasons. It makes sense we think of nature as what is outside.

The secondary definition of *nature* in the Google dictionary reads as "the basic or inherent features of something, especially when seen as characteristic of it" and is further explained as "the innate or essential qualities or character of a person or animal" and "inborn or hereditary characteristics as an influence on or determinant of personality" (Google, 2021).

This second definition is the part of us we were born with, or how we are wired. It's the facts about us that make us interesting and unique. You may like beets and Brussel sprouts or you may think they taste like dirt. You may find your best work comes when you focus first thing in the morning, or you may find it takes you a few hours to warm up before the mental juices get flowing. There is nothing right or wrong with these preferences or tendencies. They are simply part of who you are. We can choose to ignore them, much as we may ignore the birds outside of the window, but we will revel in life more if we make space for what we enjoy or works best for us and manage or eliminate what we don't prefer or doesn't work.

When I mention nature, I will be referring to both definitions. Much like reflection and action, these definitions of nature can be seen as unrelated or at least disconnected, but they also can be interrelated. How the nature outside of the window spends its day can show us how the nature inside of us can maximize our day. When we take the time to be aware of how a squirrel responds to the changing seasons, we can also become aware of when we are forcing ourselves into situations that may not be working for us for now.

For example, we can admit our lives could have elements we share in common with the squirrel's life.

What could those common elements be? We observe squirrels spend the fall burying nuts and realize it is ensuring there is food readily available during the cold winter. We can humbly admit there will be hard times in our lives, just as winter is to the squirrel, and we can reflect on how to prepare for them as best we can. We could take this literally by stocking our freezer and pantry. We could take this more figuratively and increase our savings or buy more insurance. We could broaden the application by deepening our relationships and banking on emotional support in the future.

This may seem obvious or confusing depending on whether you have considered this before or if you only explore nature as a luxury on weekends or vacations. However, I have found understanding what I prefer to do easily and how I interpret or interact with the world around me has had a profound impact on my ability to stave off burnout.

When I create that magical intersection between my process and nature's processes, I am able to lean into this new normal and experience a surge of energy to accomplish more at higher quality.

When I listen to the stress of a disconnection between my actions and how the nature inside and outside me would accomplish the task, I am prompted to choose to reflect on what would be more natural. I have found when I choose to ignore this prompting and simply push onward, I accomplish less at lower quality.

ALIGNING OUR ACTIONS WITH HOW NATURE EXCELS

I learned this about myself in my first job as an engineer. In that time, I designed a number of systems using computer-aided design. The years where I had a project on a new system, or the years we switched to a completely new software system, I was rather engaged. I enjoyed building something that had not been done before. There were other years where I was repeating old learnings in projects and it felt as if every day was the same. While to some that may feel comforting, to me it was draining.

I would often drag myself to work and sometimes felt like a failure. Was I more engaged with something new? It turns out that is something inherent to the way humans are wired. From the new car smell to the need to have the latest smartphone, humans have a fascination with the new. Novel things activate the reward system of our brains and studies have shown engaging with something new can be just as provocative as a monetary reward. This is why companies can increase sales by releasing old products with a new spin or new packaging (Swaminathan, 2008).

Whether I like it or not, I am no different and I, like a crow, am often distracted by shiny, new objects. I have said for years I want to take a class in blacksmithing just for the experience of learning something new, knowing full well I will never do it again. Just the thought of it makes me feel like a child on Christmas morning clapping my hands as someone hands me a gift. And as a child with any gift, there will come a time when the learning will lose its shine, a part will break off, and I will not be excited about it anymore.

I sat with my feeling of being drained and looked for a way through it. In my reflection, I realized there was a repeating two-year cycle. The first year was full of exploring new things. The second year was refining and mastering it to another level. If there was a third year, I only wanted to stick to it if I was transitioning out and handing something over to someone else. I didn't always have the luxury of being able to hand things off, and sometimes I had to do the drudgery of maintenance. I would often feel the life in me draining away and considered moving to a new position. I was in a time of life where I needed to stay put, so I looked for other ways of coping. I learned in those "third years" I could relieve the stress by creating change in my life, so something new was happening.

One time, I dove into using a day planner for time management. Another, I took on creating templates for the group to streamline our work. My go-to, though, was to rearrange my office. It was something I could control and it was completely about me. I can still feel the moment of internally clapping my hands when I would walk through the office door and gaze upon the new arrangement. Even though the office was not that big, I was sitting somewhere different within the space. I would discover newness in the lighting, the sounds, and the movement of others outside the door. Each discovery gave me a small reward and made me feel alive.

This revelation about myself didn't just happen overnight, and quite honestly, it only happened because I needed to find a way to cope with the stress. You could say I was forced to look at myself and find ways to actively make things better. Awareness of oneself is not something we often seek out, mostly because we think we know ourselves. Dr. Tasha Eurich, an organizational psychologist and author of *Insight: The Surprising Truth About How Others See Us, How We See Ourselves, and Why the Answers Matter More than We Think*, found through a series of surveys 95 percent of people think they are self-aware, but only a maximum of 15 percent are. Her research shows there are three main reasons why we think this way. First, we are happier when we think of ourselves positively, which can be shown through the facade of social media. Secondly, we have blind spots to any other truth. Lastly, we often spend our days on autopilot without considering what we are doing or why we are even doing it in the first place.

Dr. Eurich claims there are two types of self-awareness: internal and external. Internal self-awareness is looking inward and knowing what we value, who we want to be, and what we are passionate about. External self-awareness is looking outward and understanding what other people see when they look at us. If you interact with other people, external self-awareness is easier to come by, but that does not mean those who are externally aware are internally aware. In either case, one must be deliberate in cultivating the space to gain understanding and be brave to hear the truth—no matter how wonderful it is. This takes energy, stamina, and an eye for themes and patterns. Dr. Eurich encourages us to take the time to become self-aware (Eurich, 2017).

> "Self-awareness is absolutely worth the effort, and it helps us be more confident and more in control of our lives."
>
> — DR. TASHA EURICH, AUTHOR OF *INSIGHT* (KAUFLIN, 2017)

Coming to terms with my natural tendency to be more engaged with something new and observing that newness stayed for about two years gave me a sense of control. I could then make better decisions on how to manage my work life, such as intentionally creating change every two years whether my projects had any change or not. By being honest with myself about how what I was doing was not the best for me, I could open to the possibility of something that was better for me. I was then able to keep burnout at bay.

LOOKING TO NATURE FOR GUIDANCE

Looking to nature may help one take that first step and learn how to become more self-aware. In this case, it may be looking for tips and tricks on how nature is aware. For example, the roots of a plant go through a self-reinforcing chemical cycle that allows them to know if there is the required calcium available ahead. If there is soil, there will be calcium. If there is an obstacle such as a rock, the root will not find calcium and will stop growing in that direction even before it reaches the rock. The root does not continue until it hits the rock. It knows calcium is what it needs and senses the rock does not have any to give. It simply stops growing in that direction and redirects its effort where it can succeed (Live Science, 2021).

In other cases, nature may have answers on how to solve problems, like the woodpecker revealing to the doctors what kind of product would help prevent brain injuries. Nature also can guide us on processes by showing us when to have what activities. For millennia, humans have domesticated plants and this long-term commitment to a particular piece of land allowed humans to cultivate fruit such as apples. We have learned through this the tree has different activities depending on the season of the year.

In the spring, as the weather and ground warms, the sap flows in the trunk out to the branches to prepare for producing fruit. The trees leaf out and blossom to attract bees that pollinate the flower to bear fruit.

In the summer, the weather becomes hot and the temperatures stay warm even after the sun goes down, so the fruit grows rapidly.

In the autumn, the fruit stops growing, becomes ripe, and falls from the tree if it is not harvested. As the weather cools, the sap flows less and the tree stops nourishing the leaves to let them all fall off.

In the winter, the tree will go into dormancy and generally stop growing completely (TH Tree Services, 2021). If the temperatures drop low enough, the hormones that cause the tree to go into dormancy will break down. Without the cold, this hormone will stay and stop the flowers from budding in the spring (Grant, 2020).

While we may not enjoy it, winter is actually necessary to be able to have apples.

Nature is full of examples of how cycles of resting and producing, or reflection and action, are necessary. Reflection and action can be seen together to achieve greater things. The stories are there to open our eyes to new possibilities. There are cycles just as short as a single inhale and exhale during breathing and as long as the four seasons. There are many different options to inspire us. The key is to take the time to observe what is happening and reflect on how it applies to what we are doing in our lives.

This can seem counterintuitive for those of us in urban environments. Doesn't nature happen out in the country or in parks? For that matter, I see the birds in my backyard or the trees on my commute every day; what could I really be missing?

THE OUTCOME OF BEING INSPIRED

Whether it is inside or outside of the window, we could be missing a great deal if we do not take time to reflect on what is natural versus what is man-made or self-made. My time with Elizabeth was one I will always be grateful for in showing me the potential of what could be lost.

Elizabeth is a first-generation American. Her parents were both Mexican and established their family in Hood River, Oregon. She lost her father early in life and her mother continued as a single parent with eight children. Her mother only had an elementary education and did not speak English, so there was only so much she could do in the US. There were times when the family did not know whether they would be eating that day or not. Elizabeth began working at a young age so she could help her family and herself.

When she was sixteen, she signed up for a study abroad scholarship, pulled enough money together to buy a plane ticket, and informed her mother she was going to be an exchange student in northern Italy for six months. As she stepped off the plane in Italy, she suddenly had parents who were taking care of her. She no longer had to worry about any typical adult concerns.

On returning, she found life in Oregon was harder than she expected. Much like Engin's experience going back to Turkey in Chapter Five, Elizabeth felt disconnected from her family, friends, and school. The connections she made in Italy helped her feel worldlier, and she grew to where she did not need to belong to one particular country or place. That freedom allowed her to become an exchange student twice while she was in college. The first time she went to Spain at twenty, but the more memorable experience was the second time at twenty-three in Ecuador.

Her Ecuador experience was split into two tracks. In her first, she would live in an urban setting. Elizabeth went a couple weeks early and stayed with a friend's family in their condo in the upper-class part of the city Quito. From there, she switched to staying with the program's host family in their home in one of the slums. Placing a student in these homes helped families who were financially in need.

Trying to not get emotional, Elizabeth recalls, "I know I grew up very poor in the US, but there was a whole other level of poverty in a third world country you don't realize [there is] until you see it and live in that. I lived with them for two months, and it was me in one room and the family of four in the other room. I just felt so guilty they were all four in one room and I was in the other and I think that was the first time I was legitimately homesick in a different way."

I pressed her on that feeling of homesickness. She explained,

"I didn't lose everything, but it was a sense of feeling like you lost everything. It was almost an appreciation for what I did have. I was grateful for what my mother gave us because I knew she worked hard. But it wasn't until that moment I realized how worse off it could have been and how much we did have. There were days [in the US] where we didn't know if we were gonna eat or not, and to see another level of devastation that's significantly below that? It opened my eyes so much more. It makes you just so much more appreciative for everything."

That was just the first track. The second part of her trip was in the Amazon with healthcare workers to experience how the Waorani indigenous people lived. In this time, the group would strip down everything from the modern world, such as cellphones, electronics, and watches, so nothing would be introduced to the tribe. She was completely disconnected from even the ability to take a picture. She realized she would "just have to really live in the moment."

Rather than feeling lost, Elizabeth felt a sense of peace and freedom. The place was beautiful, unlike the slums in the city. Life was rough because everything was made by hand, but it was a simple life without the chaos of the city.

This time with the tribe allowed her to cultivate a different perspective on how things were done. She was able to see how the people used different trees and plants for graters, for creating textiles, or for medicine. She saw new ways to interact with nature for building or creating what was needed to sustain everyday life.

"I'm a figuring-it-out kind of person, but I think figuring it out in different places and constraints has really helped me have that different perspective. It creates a whole new level of light for me, and that creates a whole new level of appreciation for things that never go away. It made me so appreciative and then also kind of instilled that continuous drive."

Gratitude creates drive. Reflecting on her blessings motivated her to action. Elizabeth could have readily stayed in Ecuador and created a simple life there. The cost of living was much less, she had new friends, and she was developing skills in being able to translate between Spanish and English for healthcare workers.

However, it was her gratitude that inspired her to do better and be better. She decided to go back to the US and finish her education. Down deep, she wanted to continue exploring her world. Her experiences left her feeling empowered to change her surroundings and her circumstances. While her journey meandered through many kinds of experiences, her gratitude inspired her to keep going. She's now on her first step of a new path in a strategic role at a multi-billion-dollar company that opens up even more opportunities for her and the company to grow.

Elizabeth's story shows us we have many choices before us in creating a process for our lives. We can confine ourselves to a man-made life or we can search for a natural life that makes us feel free. The process of a natural life can range from living off the land in the middle of a forest to focusing on what makes us grateful. In any case, the outcome is we are filled with the drive to share what we have and in doing so, make the world a better place.

COMING BACK FULL CIRCLE

Left to our own devices, we as humans tend to narrow our view, and that often results in choosing a life on autopilot filled with constant action. To break ourselves out of that rut, it is best we look inside and outside ourselves to open up possibilities on how to care for ourselves by creating our own process.

Nature is a wonderful source of inspiration with its grandeur, its simplicity, and its cycles. One can see these in how we breathe, how the sun rises and sets, and how the seasons change. The cycles create a rhythm of reflection and action, of giving and taking, of producing and resting.

Nature is also a constant source of inspiration, since it tends to tease us with what it is doing in bold and subtle ways. With each mystery that is solved, there are a hundred more that open up to us to keep us engaged. Yet, there is still a symmetry that leads us in how to apply what we learn to our process.

SEVEN

Layer upon Layer

———

"Does an emerald lose its beauty for lack of admiration?"

— MARCUS AURELIUS

"Whatever anyone does or says, I must still be emerald and keep my color."

— MARCUS AURELIUS (HAMMOND, ET AL., 2019)

The anatomy of the earth is four layers: the inner core, the outer core, the mantle, and the crust. The inner core is a solid metal ball of iron and nickel located four thousand miles below the surface. The outer core is liquid iron and nickel at three thousand miles deep that moves about chaotically creating electricity that generates a magnetic field. The mantle is an eighteen-hundred-mile-thick, slow-moving liquid made of iron, magnesium, and silicon. The crust of the earth we interact with is only three to forty-three miles thick (Geiger, 2019).

Where the mantle and the crust meet is a zone of constant movement that mixes a number of different minerals and chemicals to create a unique soup. The movement in the zone also creates areas of high temperature and pressure that fracture the crust. As the soup flows into these new spaces, crystals have the chance to form, resulting in gemstone deposits (Clark, 2021).

The movement of the mantle also breaks the crust into large plates across the earth's surface that float on the liquid mantle. The plates only move about two inches a year, but that is enough to create volcanic eruptions and earthquakes that move the gemstones closer to the surface (Geiger, 2019). Then wind and rain do their work to erode the softer rock and minerals, so if we are observant, we can discover the gemstone deposit (Clark, 2021).

Gemstones moved by the volcanic eruptions are easier to find because of a large "pipe" of rock formed as the mantle flowed to the surface. Diamonds are most often found this way. Gemstones moved by colliding plates are often scattered in smaller quantities across a wider area of rock. Most colored gemstones, like emeralds, rubies, and sapphires, are found this way (Somarin, 2014).

Because of the broader distribution of colored gemstones, the mining is delicate work and much more time-consuming. Since the extra effort generally does not result in substantial profit, large industrial mining companies leave these deposits for smaller companies that often use manual labor (Somarin, 2014). One of these—Gemfields Mining Company in the UK—has taken a unique approach to increase the likelihood of success not only for the business, but also for the earth and the surrounding community as well (Gemfields, 2021).

Their approach begins with a thorough appraisal of the deposit for the existence of gemstones and for the quality and value of the deposit long before the mining begins. The Kagem Emerald Mine in northern Zambia was assessed with data from aerial photos of over forty-one square miles to determine possible areas to find the emeralds. The surveyors then moved in to systematically sample the ground in 913 holes and created a library of ninety-four thousand meters of rock. With that knowledge, a three-dimensional model of the mine was created to allow the company to estimate 1.8 billion carats exist there and to inform a twenty-five-year long-term strategy that included a designed plan on the best way to extract the gems (Gemfields, 2021b; Gemfields, 2021c).

Knowing there was a possibility of a good business, the impact of the work on the community and environment were assessed and buy-in from the international, national, and local communities was sought. Gemfields then also determined what would be needed to create a healthy community so there was a workforce to continue to support the business. They made such investments as installing healthcare facilities, schools for children and their parents, and farming projects so the people would be healthier overall (Gemfields, 2021a).

Nature has spent millions to billions of years creating gemstones. The ability for humans to enjoy these gemstones requires a great deal of work reading the earth for where they are and uncovering layer upon layer of material to bring them out to the light of day. When we are developing our own processes and looking to nature for our inspiration, it would be best if we kept in mind there is a great deal to be explored below the surface. If we are patient and take the time to do so, there is something beautiful and precious that waits for us to discover it.

VALUE AND CELEBRATE THE WORK IN PROGRESS

When emeralds are taken from the mine, they are certainly not what one would expect to have in a tiara, necklace, or ring. While there is a lot of work to find and bring the emeralds out of the mine, there could be as much, if not more, work to remove the minerals from around the emerald crystals. In the Gemfield's Kagem Mine, quartz surrounds the emeralds. The quartz is removed by trimming or cobbing it away by hand millimeter by millimeter. One of the most famous stones, Gemfield's Medusa emerald, was created by this process and the emerald crystals were left in the shape and direction they were formed as an example of a natural specimen (Gaboury, 2021; Pardieu, 2011).

We can readily imagine the lapidarist taking a raw crystal and cutting, grinding, and polishing it into a beautiful shape. We may even jump from there to visit a jeweler who sets the stone into a work of art with diamonds and gold. We can all agree the crystals have gone through step upon step of processing to get to the point where it may even sit in my jewelry box at home. The question for me is at what step is the stone considered valuable?

When is an emerald an emerald?

I would agree beauty is in the eye of the beholder and a wise person would be able to see an emerald in the rough. This is when looking beyond the surface becomes important, just as knowing where we are in the process as each layer is removed is also important. Gemfields would assign value to the rocks they pull out of the mine, just as they would to the rough-cut pieces they create through the trimming and cobbing processes. They are all valuable steps to get to the piece of jewelry, and if we ignore those steps, then the enjoyment of processing the emerald is lost.

I have learned we can say the same when we are developing and working our own process. If we do not acknowledge the work we have accomplished at each of the steps and assign a value to it, we will have a hard time continuing all the steps until we get to the most valuable treasure at the end. It helps to see the beauty of where we are and know it is invaluable to where we are going.

In hindsight, I have had a number of moments in my life where I have not taken the time to peel back all the layers to discover what lay beneath. When I start a project, I have a vision of where it is going and even a high-level definition of success. As I meander through the work, the details flesh and morph the vision out. No matter the path I take, though, when I realize the vision, I consider the project complete.

That isn't always the truth. Often, that is not a big deal, but I do find when I mentally have checked anything off my list and later have to put it back on the list, a growl begins to emerge from somewhere deep inside. I believe this is why I hate maintenance tasks. They keep turning back up.

There are times, though, when putting something back on the list will derail me. For example, say I am working with a few people on planning an event. Together we have developed a task list and everyone volunteers for various tasks. At some point, a colleague looks at my list and comments I have taken on too much. I take a look and while I know I could manage it, it would be easier if I did not have all of it. She readily suggests she will take on the catering and I am grateful I can focus on the graphics for the posters.

Time passes. My task list is being well managed and I am able to relax and enjoy myself. Two weeks before the event, the group reconvenes to check how things are going and my colleague has not been able to handle the catering. The task moves back to my list and I now feel I am in a pressure cooker. What bothers me most is I could have managed my time if the catering was on my list from the beginning. It was putting it back on my list that caused all the issues and my lost sense of control.

Managing my task list has been something I have both failed and excelled at throughout my life. With every career change, I have found a growth opportunity when I approach task lists. One such time was when I transitioned from engineering to design. Iterations of prototypes are a mainstay of the design process. This philosophy pushed me to open up mentally to make room for incompleteness. In fact, one mentor of mine said the greatest issue for designers is the attitude the work can always be improved, so it can become hard for a designer to let go of the project, since in their mind it is never truly done. I laughed out loud because I thought engineers had the corner on the market for adding on more and more.

At first, I saw the iterations as repeating work and tried my best to minimize the number of prototypes by planning well and only changing the resolution between prototypes. It was only when I was interacting with and presenting the prototypes I realized something more could be gained. By watching the user get confused with how to pick up a prototype or how to store the product, I was able to see how many more iterations I needed to determine all the features the user needed and desired.

Another time of growth has been in writing this book. In conversations with my development editor, Whitney, I made a number of parallels between creating in design and creating in writing. I knew the stories I would send to her were prototypes and she would see how useful they were for the project. We sorted, created, revised, and edited.

At one point, we were facing the deadline for submitting a first draft. I looked at what there was to do and set forward to make it happen. I completed the first draft of everything we discussed and had it in her hands early. It was a great feeling. Whitney congratulated me and exclaimed, "You have written a book!" In my mind, the first draft was complete. I checked it off my list.

Whitney's words were true, but in looking back, I am not certain I absorbed them. I have never been an aspiring author, so I also do not have years of knowledge in how to be an author. To me, a book is when there is something to purchase at the store or on my Kindle. So, to me, a first draft was just a step. Still, how many people make it that far? In the beginning of the project, we were told only 2 percent of people who start will actually finish writing a book. Another statistic floating around the Internet says 3 percent (Zink, 2021). In any case, I hung up the call with Whitney and went on as if it was any other day.

It was two weeks before I officially submitted the first draft to the publishing house. Whitney had made a number of suggestions, and I decided to use that time to work on those. One of the suggestions was to take one chapter and split it into three. In fact, this is the second of those three chapters. The first of the three went very well and I toyed with the idea of completing these chapters before the official submission.

As I started to pull the words apart and look for other stories to make the points needed, the optimism started to fall away and the book started to feel incomplete. In a way, my idea of completing these three chapters placed the first draft back on my task list. I literally had not even given myself a full day to bask in the joy of completion before I redefined "complete" and snuck it back on the list. A low-level growl sat in my gut for that whole week.

When I finally realized what I had done, I stopped and asked myself why. I know this is just a first draft and there will be at least three more drafts coming. I know iterations are needed to get to something wonderful, just like there must be layers of rock removed to find the gemstones. Why was the growl present? Why was I not enjoying myself? The answer from my reflection was I had not stopped to accept that accomplishment. Deep down, I still assumed the only definition of complete was the one where the book was printed on paper with a hardcover. So, while I said "complete" and told that growling tiger I had checked it off my list, I really didn't believe it.

Layers or iterations are an important part of a process that works toward something valuable. Planning for those iterations is essential to reaching those goals.

> Working that plan can create results, but it is important to realize acknowledging stages of completion and celebrating the accomplishments along the way are even more necessary than the planning itself.

We can then look at our list and move to the next phase filled with possibility.

NATURE HAS STORIES TO TELL

Layers of rock and gemstones make for a good metaphor on how we can look deeper to find something valuable. The issue is other examples within nature can be elusive, and it is helpful to look to an expert on how we can find the deeper meaning. I met such an expert in Stacy Levy, an environmental artist from Pennsylvania.

Stacy Levy came from a family of artists, so many she avoided becoming one, feeling she would carry more cachet in the sciences. But she could not connect to pure science. She wanted her work to be something people would want to experience.

As she identified this passion, she was able to connect with urban forestry because she saw how her knowledge of ecology could make a space not only accessible, but an entrancing beauty created to attract people.

Her first projects were to restore urban forests through the mid-Atlantic. Growth of the forest was so tremendous in these areas that invasive species, such as bittersweet or cat-brier, created blankets over the trees. Her work was to go in with a pole saw and pruners cutting away the vines by hand to give the forest space to spring back into its own sylvan architecture. As she removed layer after layer, she unveiled majestic oaks, red maples, and flowering dogwoods, much like a fashion designer revealing their spring collection.

Looking back, Levy realized even as a forester she could not escape her family's DNA and was still becoming an artist. It was the time in urban forestry that taught her how to envision the multiple dimensions and layers of a large-scale project, and to be able to create enduring experiences. Her intent was to help people connect with the natural processes that surround them. In normal, hectic urban life, it is easy to miss what is happening outside in nature. Levy creates visual metaphors to help the public perceive "what is too small to be seen, too invisible to be considered, or too vast to be understood" (Levy, 2021a).

One can see her work *Tampa Wind* on the tower of the Environmental Sciences Building at the University of South Florida, where three thousand stainless steel discs were suspended to reflect the sky, clouds, and surroundings as they responded to the movement of the wind and the falling of the rain (Levy, 2021b). Or head to St. Petersburg, Russia, to see *Rose Level*, where trees in an urban park were wrapped in pink surveyor's tape to tangibly show what would be underwater if the park were flooded from rising sea levels (Levy, 2021c).

To explain the point of her art, she gave us an illustration we can all comprehend. One can notice the leaves change their colors. Because of experience, one knows the leaves used to be green and those on the ground used to be on the trees. Levy's point was that without that knowledge, we only have the colored leaves on the ground. Nature was working in the moment where it was and the moment then was just a snapshot of a bigger picture. Or as Levy says, "Nature hides what it is doing" (Science History Institute, 2013). In a way, those with the curiosity were given a mystery to solve.

In an example of this, Levy described seeing a series of incidents in the canvas of a blanket of snow.

> *"You can see entire events in snow. Snow is like a huge piece of landscape paper. One afternoon, I saw a perfect rendition of a hawk's wing imprinted in the snow. How did that happen? Then a couple more holes of distributed snow over there...and then some blood drops in the snow. And then you realized the hawk came down, landing on something like a mouse, scrambling to get this mouse—tumbling in the snow and obviously caught it. A whole story unfolded like a forensics story because it was embossed in the snow, and you could see every step of the process...If it all happened in one place that [hawk] landed, dug, wrestled, and killed all*

in one core, you would have had to dig down to get it,
but because it happened [from] here to here to here, you
could see this story" (Science History Institute, 2013).

That is Stacy Levy's intention with her work, to pull out nature's stories that surround each of us so we have the chance to see it, appreciate it, consider it, and maybe even learn something new from it.

TRACK NATURE'S STORY

This is also our work in developing our own process. Just as Levy pulls out the natural processes in an urban environment, we are looking for what is naturally happening in the built environment of our lives. We have a man-made structure we confine ourselves to, assuming nature happens in some faraway place and forgetting nature is happening right beside and inside us. When we finally realize what is happening, we have the opportunity to see it, appreciate it for what it is, consider if we want to make more of it, and create something new for ourselves from it. To understand what this could look like, I researched more on Levy's work and was intrigued by what I found.

In 2015, Philadelphia was experiencing a planning renaissance and chose to make a large investment in its parks, trails, and public spaces. One area of focus was the Bartram's Garden, a forty-five-acre oasis in southwest Philly and on the western bank of the Schuylkill River. Despite being a National Historic Landmark, being next to Drexel University, and being a short commute from City Hall, the garden was considered unknown. The proposal was to create a connection between the garden and the surrounding neighborhood, and to use art and horticulture to encourage those neighborhoods to connect to each other. Out of this, Art@Bartram's was created to install public art within and around the garden in a multi-year effort lead by Mural Arts Philadelphia, the nation's largest public art program dedicated to promoting engagement in communities (Lindy, 2021; Mural Arts, 2021a).

Levy was from Pennsylvania and was a natural choice to participate. In the spring of 2016, she was awarded the first of the installations. Levy's favorite medium was water and water flows, so she readily focused on the connection Bartram's Garden had with Schuylkill River and hoped to encourage visitors to engage with the river (Mural Arts Philadelphia, 2021).

Levy created a series of strings of multicolored buoys that drew attention to the river and named the work *Tide Field*. At high tide, each string of buoys stood upright with only the top three red spheres showing. As the tide went out, the buoy started to bend over and eventually, all three red buoys and three teal-colored buoys were visible. At low tide, the entire string of nine spheres floated on the surface of the water and the three colors of red, teal, and green all could be seen. In this horizontal state, the buoys then danced with the surface of the water in ways that would be otherwise unobserved. The cycle of the tide was revealed. With experience, one could get a sense of a dependable timetable.

Levy spent two years developing the installation. Her first step was spending time with the water to discover the natural stories she wanted to track.

"The tide ebbs and flows in the city on its own schedule, influenced by the gravitational pull of the moon and sun. It runs on a timetable all its own—unaffiliated with human schedules. The tidal fluctuation of the Schuylkill gives us a sense of the enduring quality of natural processes, occurring in the midst of our human world of concrete and steel. Having an understanding of the tidal timing and amplitude is a first step in creating a kinship with the river."

The tide is not the only force moving the water. "Wind currents pull in one direction, the actual river currents in another direction, tide in a third direction, and there are micro areas of eddies affected by other things, like the topography of the river bed. There is a myriad of things," said Levy. "The more time I spend on water, the more mysteries arise" (stacylevyART, 2018).

Similar to the falling autumn leaves, any observation is simply a snapshot of that moment.

Nature's cycles can be bold or subtle, and in spending time observing and interacting with that cycle, one can start to unravel the secrets of what it is accomplishing. The riddles are worth investigating to help us use the learnings as metaphors for our own lives. The interesting part, though, Levy teaches us is there are layers of mystery. Just as we detect one layer and peel it back, we reveal another layer. As Levy leads with her art, we are first called to know about nature in and outside of our lives. With that knowledge, we can come to care about our lives and develop a process that will enable us to care for ourselves.

As we develop our processes, we need to understand there are layers of depth not only to what we mimic, but to how we apply the inspirations. The amount and depth of reflection, action, and combinations of the two can vary within and between layers. We will be constantly learning not only about the layer we are in, but what the next layer is about. It is wise then to be grateful for how far we've come, where we are, and the potential for where we can go.

EIGHT

Finding Patterns in Nature

———

> *"It is not enough to be busy. So are the ants. The question is: what are we busy about?"*
>
> — HENRY DAVID THOREAU (AZ QUOTES, 2021)

Think about the last time you moved furniture, say a couch through a doorway. It is not something you would choose to attempt on your own. You solicit a couple of friends to help. You lift one end and a friend lifts the other. When you reach the door, there is a debate about how to orient the couch to get it through. You all may try some way, determine it isn't working, back up, and try another way. A third friend suggests using the back door. It's frustrating and time-consuming and makes most of us swear next time, we will pay professionals.

Ants are professional movers in their world. They are able to get the job done by being amazing collaborators and problem solvers. Jacob Wilde told a story at TEDxQueensU of being on an entomology course in India and was asked to come back from the field with observations of how insects solve problems.

He came across weaver ants building a nest between two halves of a leaf they had sewn together. He sliced the seam open to observe the response. The ants, of course, went crazy running everywhere. Soon, the weaver ants lined up their bodies to create a number of long chains. They pulled the edge of one side of the leaf back over to touch the other. A number of individual ants stepped up to hold the two edges together, looking much like the pins of a zipper. Another group of ants brought the ant larvae that excrete a silk. The adult ants would "sew" the leaf together by drawing the larvae silk from one edge to the other and back again.

Jacob was excited about the experience, but realized it was a repeat of what the ants would do naturally and not necessarily problem-solving. To create a problem, he cut an irregular shape out of the middle of the leaf. The ants went back to forming long chains across the opening and attempted to pull the edges together to no avail. Three ants wandered to the forest floor and found the piece of the leaf Jacob had cut out. One started to move it back to the nest. The other two noticed and joined in to help. They brought it back to the hole Jacob had cut. A number of ants swooped in, moved it around until it was oriented correctly, and sewed the edges of the piece shut (TEDx Talks, 2018).

Observations such as these have made researchers dig further into how ants solve problems. Ants often find the optimal path between the nest and a food source. Researchers have taken that further by releasing ants in a maze to let them find the optimal path. From this knowledge, computer scientists were able to create a method called ant colony optimization to help software solve problems.

The issue with the method is how the software handles change. The algorithm would find the optimal path and forget about all the other options so when something changed, the program would get caught spinning in a loop or get lost after wandering off the path. This is how cellphone calls can be dropped.

Fortunately, biologists continued working with the ants. Researchers found when they altered the maze geometry to discourage the ants from the old optimal path, the ants modified the original path slightly to continue through the maze, but within a short period, the collective was able to find a new optimal path that was more efficient (Holm, 2010).

The beauty was in the face of the change, the ants didn't continue pushing the same path that was now not working. They kept their focus on solving the maze and simply worked to improve the efficiency. This is the leap the algorithms needed to handle complex and dynamic problems.

We have talked about looking to nature for inspiration on developing our processes, and even explored there are layers of depth to continually inform us. When we are engaging with nature, it is also good to look for the patterns that are created, much like the patterns the ants would make through the maze. These can be small or large and can come from many sources, but these patterns can help us understand how to apply what we are learning to make optimal and robust processes.

ANALYZING THE PATTERN OF CYCLES

With all of these options and variables and layers, it can be difficult to know where to start and how to choose the "right" pattern. What may help is to look for commonalities as we observe new areas of nature. For example, when I look at the pattern of cycles, there is a beginning, a middle, and an end that are repeated over and over. That by itself allows one to define what is the beginning and the end. That also means there is a point of transition between the repeats that allows for a moment of decision or change.

Think about breathing. Take a deep breath in and then let it out. Traditionally, we say inhale before exhale and imply we begin by breathing in. There is nothing that says you cannot start the definition of the cycle with exhaling. In either case, though, there is a point where the breath transitions from filling to emptying and in that moment, the breath could be held.

This point of change could be a helpful feature in our processes. It creates as an opportunity for us to make a decision. Cultivating a process that allows us to have control can be very powerful across our lives. If we look for other features of cycles, are there other powerful moments we could employ?

As I researched cycles, I found eight distinct phases. A good example is the apple tree through the seasons. The tree *receives* the warmth of spring and *prepares* for making apples by leafing out and flowering. The flowers attract bees for pollination and the apples are *produced*. The heat of the summer allows for the apples to *refine*. When complete, the apples can be *harvested*. The weather will turn cooler and the tree will *let go* of its leaves so it can *rest* during the winter. When the weather turns cold enough, the hormones creating the dormancy are broken down so the tree is prepared to *begin again* when spring comes (Grant, 2021; TH Trees, 2021). In this case, the eight phases are receiving, preparing, producing, refining, harvesting, letting go, resting, and beginning again.

The purpose of the phases in this example is rather clear to me, but when I look at other cycles, I may see the eight phases, but not necessarily the purpose of the phases. For example, the earth's moon can be described as having eight phases based on the amount of light reflecting on the moon's surface. At least in the US, the phases start with the new moon, where there is no illumination due to the earth blocking out the sun. From there, the amount of surface that is lit grows though a waxing crescent moon phase until it is half-illuminated at the first quarter moon. The amount of light continues to grow through the waxing gibbous phase to the full moon phase we notice the most. Then the phases continue through the waning gibbous, the third quarter, and the waning crescent as the amount of light recedes back to the new moon.

What is in common is the idea of eight phases between the apple tree example and the moon example. What is different is the time scale and the outcome of the phases. The tree follows the seasons to produce apples at one point and the moon varies in how it illuminates the darkness of our skies. Focusing on the commonalities and the differences, we have the opportunity to place the concepts side by side and overlap the two to create something new. What if we took the purposes of the apple tree over the seasons and used the moon phases as a timepiece to create one process for each month or moon?

If we were to try this, the new moon can be about receiving, the waxing crescent about preparing, the first quarter producing, the waxing gibbous refining, the full moon harvesting, the waning gibbous sharing, the last quarter on letting go, and the waning crescent on resting to begin again. Here is a good framework for a process that allows for a distinct theme for each phase and a reasonable time frame. What is missing is the application, and that is left up to each of us as we decide what we want to accomplish as we use our processes.

For me, I am seeking a process to help me design a life I love where what I work on matters to me in a way that supports and encourages me to be healthy. For me then, I apply the moon phases in this way. The new moon can be about *receiving* my inner wisdom on what my heart truly desires. The waxing crescent moon is about *preparing* for making that a reality. The first quarter moon I *produce* the first attempt at that reality. The waxing gibbous moon is for *refining* that attempt. During the full moon, I *harvest* the insights as to how well my heart's desire is met. The waning gibbous moon prompts for a time of *sharing* the bounty of the harvest. The last quarter moon is a time to *let go* of what is not going well. The waning crescent moon is a time of *rest* so I can *begin again* with the next cycle.

With this example, the eight commonalities are present, but there is something new in the sharing of the harvest. This may be implied with the idea of a tree sharing the apple as it is harvested, but with the moon cycle, one can be more intentional about the time of sharing. The intentionality is something that resonates with me and is one reason I have been attracted to using the moon cycle as a timepiece.

I gave myself 2020 to try this way of working. Overall, this has been a great structure that has allowed me to not only designate times of action and times of reflection, but also the change between phases allows for a decision point. Is this project working? Do I want to continue in this way? What came out of this that was useful?

I found that could be helpful during the moon, but it was also a good idea to check in once a season to see how I felt over multiple moons. If there was a trend, then I knew a change in my process needed to happen. Since it was my first attempt at the reviews each season, these were rather awkward, but I did find the purposes of the apple tree changing with the seasons would nag at me. I was using the apple tree purposes within the moon phase, but somehow each moon looked the same, and it felt rather like I was cutting out cookies.

After a couple of reviews, I realized I felt different with the seasons. I would want to get out and do more in the spring and I would grow those new things in the summer, but in the fall, I was ready to start pulling back from anything new. In the winter, I just wanted to bundle up and stay warm. It occurred to me to plan my year to take advantage of how I felt so I could have a better year overall. For 2021, I am now taking the purposes of the apple tree and applying those as a theme to the whole moon. January is for dreaming, February is for preparing, and so on.

As I am working this process within a process, I am also seeing how I can connect the moons together to create a larger group of projects that have even more impact. I also am able to dream bigger as I look at how I want to be in a year. It gives me greater hope and peace than I even had in 2020. Being able to see I can apply the cycle pattern from the apple tree to other time scales is now making me curious about my individual days. I wonder if there is a similar rhythm, but that is a project for another time.

As we develop our processes, it will take some trial and error to find what is right for us. Some initial observations into nature will help us get on the right track to something that will work but taking the time to identify patterns and analyze what they mean to us will connect what we try more deeply with who we are. That can give us confidence and hope that the process will help us to increase the meaning of what we are working on, and the effort will take us to where we want to go.

RESEARCHING YOURSELF

The key to being able to apply the patterns we see in nature to our own process is understanding our unique natural tendencies. I learned not only this from Catalina, and also that sometimes these tendencies are so strong we apply them without even knowing it.

I met with Catalina during the quarantine in 2020. She, like me, had a career and then chose to pursue an advanced degree in design. I knew from my own experience in working on a Master's in Industrial Design that going back to school later in life caused one to spend time focusing on being more efficient, and this required moments of self-observation to understand what worked and what didn't. It had been four years since I was in the throes of it, but I was hopeful Catalina would have a fresh view since she was in the middle of a doctorate program.

She told me the first big difference between the Master's and the PhD program is a semester-long course called Research Paradigms in Design, specifically created to help students understand what kind of researchers they were (NCSU Wolfware, 2021). Two of the approaches to research are qualitative and quantitative. Qualitative is often associated with words and would be focused on observations of feelings, experiences, and stories (Creswell, 2014). Brené Brown's research on how the fear of being disconnected from others convinces people they are unlovable is a good example of a *qualitative* research (Brown, 2021). Quantitative is often associated with numbers and would be focused on what can be measured, such as force, weights, or percentages (Creswell, 2014). Marie Curie's laboratory experiments to determine how to isolate the radioactive chemicals of polonium and radium are good examples of a *quantitative* research (The Nobel Prize, 2021).

These kinds of research are not distinctly separate from each other but are opposites on a spectrum. There are many researchers who combine these approaches to explore a larger story. How one chooses where you are on the spectrum and thereby what methods you will use depends upon your worldview. Researchers can select from a number of worldviews, such as constructivism and positivism. Constructivists understand there can be multiple meanings from the data's interpretation, and these researchers generate theories from the interpretations. Positivists already have an established theory and are conducting research to confirm or deny the theory (Creswell, 2014).

In this class, Catalina discovered she was a constructivist and described herself as one who "constructs knowledge on what she observes in the world." This was the most interesting part of transitioning from a Master's to a PhD for her. After going through this class, Catalina felt she had been misusing the word "research." During her Master's, she felt everything she did was research. If she was reading articles, it was research. Anything she did to absorb information was research. However, when she heard the definitions in class, she realized there were distinct differences between qualitative and quantitative research. While she naturally took in information like a qualitative researcher, she began to understand how the numbers and statistics would open up whole new worlds to her. She realized she had a number of new tools in her toolbox and she was excited at the possibility.

To me, this was a blending of intuition and logic, and for that matter, it was also a blending of reflection and action. I asked her how that was working for her. Catalina responded, "My initial intentions for research are always driven by emotion. When I'm the one picking the topic, I always find myself asking the question, 'Where did I feel frustrated?' and that drives me. Most of my research, I am always trying to improve the issues that cause these frustrations."

She went on by telling me of a project for an anthropology class where students practice ethnographic qualitative research methods they can later use in their dissertation research. The assignment was to research a group of people who were all alike.

One of the methods they used was 'participant observation,' where the researcher goes into the field and immerses themselves as one of the research participants. This gave her a chance to practice switching back and forth between experiencing for herself and observing the other participants. While other students chose to study groups from their karate class to online gamers, Catalina chose something very personal. She was in the middle of her own grief process from losing her husband a couple of months back and decided to study young widows.

Catalina joined a grief support group. There she shared her grief and felt those emotions, but she could not stay there with it. As soon as another participant would start sharing, she flipped the switch from crying like a baby as a participant to taking notes as a researcher. Catalina was a very rational person and felt talking about her emotions was hard. Talking about others' emotions was quite easy because she rationalized it, but it was a different story when she was the one experiencing the feelings.

She told of how there were times where she thought she was going crazy. There was the time she was standing at the ATM trying to remember the four-digit code she'd had her whole life. The number simply would not come forward. Then there was the time she forgot to pick up her kids. She started to tell herself she was a bad mom and was losing her mind.

"I was having a really rough time with it, but once I was able to remove myself from the situation and look at it as a researcher, I was able to figure out, 'Oh God, I'm not crazy. This is happening to everybody.' All of these things I am telling you saved my life, because I was able to understand the grief process as a step-by-step thing."

She was able to see that dark cold place she found herself in was just a phase, and she could move through it to the other side. Observing others, she understood she was the only one who could get herself out of that place. One of the insights she found through this study was there was a group of women who reinvented themselves either by embracing new hobbies, starting a new business, meeting new people, or opening themselves to a new relationship. These reinvented women seemed to be happier and were able to move forward more successfully than those who didn't. Personally, Catalina decided to give dating a chance. Although in her heart it felt as if she would never be ready, she knew if she didn't try, she never would. So, she started meeting people and began to explore the possibility of a happy life beyond her own loss.

Catalina readily applied these tools to her dissertation. She was interested in healthcare because she had grown up in a household of doctors. The only reason she did not go into medicine herself was because the sight of blood made her faint. So instead, she became passionate about how to create better medical devices and experiences to influence medical outcomes. Being a researcher, though, she wanted to take that further and develop methods and tools for all designers.

She sat down in the spring semester of 2020 with her advisor to flesh out what part of healthcare to research, and they both realized they were looking at a once-in-a-lifetime event with the global pandemic. Prior methods and tools were going to need an enormous shift to be able to handle the new normal, and the use of telehealth would become a real option for everyone since social distancing was one of the main strategies to contain the virus.

She had started with the user experience of patients, caregivers, and doctors during the pandemic to understand what was working and where there were opportunities for improvement. With that understanding, she was then ready to engage with experts to ideate on what the future of telehealth would be after the global lockdown. Would the world go back to the first version of healthcare or would there be a more blended model? Finally, she was planning to work with that forecast in mind to hypothesize what the role of designers could be in fleshing out that new normal.

Catalina intentionally took time to look for patterns in her own life so she could understand her tendencies and in turn gained knowledge in how she processes information and emotions. She looked to others who may be like her to understand tools and tricks she may want to adopt. She was then able to take her learnings and experiences, develop a process, and apply it all to her projects. As we develop our own processes, we can learn from Catalina in accepting our own innate nature, celebrating it, and even using it when we are not sure where we are or where we are going. Trusting who we are and developing a process based on that trust will take us out of even the darkest places, whether they be of grief or of burnout.

RESERVING JUDGMENT

It is one thing to find and analyze patterns. It is another thing to apply these patterns and make them stick to our lives. To know if the pattern was effective, we need to decide if the pattern was of any use. Did it work for us? And if it didn't work for us, what went wrong? We can gain some insight into this as Jacob Wilde applied what he learned about the weaver ants repairing the hole in the leaf to the roles of how people solve problems (TEDx Talks, 2018).

Jacob began the discussion by splitting people into two groups: the idea generators and the idea implementers. The idea generators were like the ants that went wandering off, found the piece of leaf on the ground, and drug it back to the nest. The idea implementers were the ones that worked tirelessly to repair the hole with the piece of leaf that was found. When ideas don't work, we often assume one of these two groups made a mistake. The idea must have not been that good or the person implementing it didn't work hard enough.

Jacob submitted there is a third group that is essential to the success of an idea. There was one ant that saw the piece of leaf as the solution and started dragging the piece back to the nest. There were others who saw the effort and chose to come and support it. These recognized taking the piece to the nest was a good idea. He applied the learning saying as we brainstorm, there is the generation of a number of ideas of varying quality and application. At some point, we must sift through all the ideas and choose which will be implemented. At this point, we must make a judgment trying to predict which of the ideas will work out in the future.

Jacob gave an example. After shopping at the grocery store, we were ready to check out and needed to choose which of the lines to join. We first looked at the shortest lines and then at how many items people ahead had in their cart. We dug deeper to understand how fast the cashier was moving today, or considered what items were easier to check out. If it turned out the line we chose didn't get us out faster, what do we blame? In that case, we considered we chose the "wrong" line (the judgment). What we didn't do was blame ourselves for wanting to check out faster (the idea) or that we spent a lot of energy analyzing the people, time, and items (the implementation) (TEDx Talks, 2018).

Our ideas are not perfect or fully formed. They need refinement and revisions before they are implemented. There is a large number of process steps between the ideas and the actions to apply the ideas, such as how to choose, improve, and execute. This is a crucial element to a complete process.

As we look for patterns in nature that will inspire how we develop our processes, we can come up with a number of ideas on how to move forward. It is helpful to remember while the ideas vary in quality, the choosing and the refining of the ideas can have as much impact on our success as the effort we put into implementing it. Our choices can be made based on a number of filters, but certainly one should be what our innate tendencies are, since that will likely allow us to accept the new normal more readily.

PART THREE

DESIGNING REFLECTION INTO YOUR LIFE

NINE

Becoming a Natural Reflector

"Life's not a race; it's a catwalk. It's not about being the first all the time; it's about being confident of where you are."

— ANONYMOUS (VERBRUGGEN, 2021)

In September of 1998, Alexander McQueen, a popular British fashion designer, revealed his spring collection. This particular show, *No. 13*, is famous for being more performance art than fashion show. With each new item in the collection, McQueen lulled the audience into a sense of calm before the final model, Shalom Harlow, in a multi-layered paper dress, strutted alone to a circular platform in the middle of the catwalk. While the platform slowly rotated, Harlow flailed her arms above her as two car-painting robots, like hissing cobras, sprayed her dress with graffiti (Mower, 2018).

With this ending, it was hard for anyone to remember the first model out on the runway was Aimee Mullins, who began the show with a brown leather corset, a cream lace skirt, and six-inch high wooden Louis XVI boots hand-carved with flowers, vines, and leaves (AnOther, 2015; Calaway, 1999). The Icelandic singer songwriter Björk was in the front row of the audience and able to get a close look at the boots. She thought they were beautiful and went backstage to touch them.

With that one touch, Björk was convinced she wanted a pair. She just needed to know what it felt like to wear them. Björk asked Mullins if the wood hurt her ankles as she walked. Mullins looked back in amazement. She had walked closely in front of Björk a couple of times in the show. How could she not know these weren't boots? Could Björk not see they were prosthetics? Mullins had been born with no fibulas and had both of her legs amputated below her knee when she was one year old. Mullins collected herself and pulled her knee out of the wood. The two "just stood there looking at each other, shocked" (Calaway, 1999).

This was not the first time Mullins had shattered expectations by just being herself. Two years earlier, she competed in the 1996 Atlanta Paralympics to set the world record in the two hundred meters at 34.06 seconds after only competing for two years in track and field (Calaway, 1999). She also was the first ever in the world to try out the carbon fiber spring prosthetics (TED, 1998).

Mullins has never considered herself disabled. In her 2009 TEDMED Talk, she tells the room of doctors, "There's been a shift in my thinking over time. If you'd asked me at fifteen years old if I would have traded prosthetics for flesh and bone legs, I wouldn't have hesitated for a second. I aspired to that kind of normalcy back then. If [the doctor] asked me today, I'm not so sure. It's because of the experiences I've had with them, not in spite of the experiences I've had with them" (TED, 2009).

Mullins took what she was given and adapted. She did not avoid the challenge of being without legs from the knee down. She leaned into it and looked for ways she could live life to the fullest. We can be certain not everything worked perfectly for her, but she started with a first step, learned from the experience, adapted what she was doing, tried again, and kept going until she made it. I can imagine she is still seeking out and adapting to new experiences today.

As we talked about in the cult of action, there will be those who see us as weak or incapable by not going along with the status quo. When we choose to develop our own processes, the same will wonder why anyone would do that. We can be seen as outsiders who should stay away from the limelight. Who are we to define and achieve success in a different way?

As we move to developing our own process, we can shut out these naysayers and be inspired by Aimee Mullins to boldly create an authentic life for ourselves. We have the choice to consider ourselves capable of anything. We can accept the challenge of being different. In fact, we can lean into it and live our fullest life. Certainly, there will be moments where our experience is less than perfect, but if we simply take the first step and try, we have much to learn on what and how to adapt so we can reach the success we desire.

Ultimately, our process should be something that supports living our best life and not something that limits our capabilities. If we can apply the principles of this book in an open way and be prepared to adapt as needed, we may take ourselves exactly where we'd planned to go or, like Mullins, we may also suddenly find ourselves on a catwalk showing the world how doing things differently makes us absolutely fabulous.

WHEN YOU KNOW YOU'VE MADE IT

Like Mullins, one must be brave to do something differently than what is expected by those around you. There can be encouraging moments that reveal themselves and serve as lampposts along the way. It is good to watch for these as we develop our own process to know we have made it. Mullins tells a story at TED2009 about what one of these encouraging moments meant to her.

After Mullins walked the catwalk for Alexander McQueen, she worked with Matthew Barney in his film called the *Cremaster 3* where they made a set of clear, glasslike legs, another set out of soil with potato and beet roots growing in them, and finally a set of cheetah legs to refer to her athletic career.

These designs were not just about function, but also about beauty and whimsy. The experience helped her look at her prosthetics differently. She realized there was much more that could happen; in fact, anything could happen in that space between her knee and the floor.

When it came time to make more humanlike prosthetics, she expanded her collection much like one would buy different shoes. Some legs were for flats and others were for heels, but with *Cremaster 3*, she also realized she could change her height by changing legs.

One particular pair let her be six foot one. She excitedly wore those to a party the first night she could. A good friend was there who knew Mullins at her "normal" height of five foot eight.

The friend's mouth dropped open. "But you're so tall!"

Mullins replied, "I know, it's a bit like wearing stilts, but I [am] having fun with it."

Her friend looked at her seriously. "But Aimee, that's not fair! It's not fair you can change your height as you want it!"

Mullins then knew people had come around to her way of thinking. She never thought she was disabled. She knew her potential and now she heard society saw she had an advantage by doing things differently (TED, 2009b).

There will be times as we develop our process when people will disregard what we are doing. There is no need to explain to those why or how we are creating our own process. The best thing for us is to keep collecting different ways of doing things, determining what is serving us well, and focusing on how to live the best life we can. Hopefully at some point, we will have fun with it. That's when we know we have made it. We are moving our life forward and loving every minute of it.

One day, as others realize what we are doing creates a benefit, we can then, if we choose to, have a discussion.

WHEN YOU KNOW YOUR PROCESS MEANS SOMETHING

It must be comforting to have people agree with or even be jealous when we are attempting something new and different. There can be the beginning of a connection that propels us all forward. That is something good for those of us feeling a bit isolated when developing our own processes, but is that all there is—a good feeling?

On *The Moth Radio Hour*, Mullins tells a story of a five-year-old girl she met in 2009 who was born with brittle bone disease that caused her left leg to be seven centimeters shorter than her right leg. The girl went through a number of treatments and surgeries, but the results did not give her the life she wanted.

She searched for "new legs" and Google came back with a number of images, including Mullins' prosthetics. She laid these pictures before her parents and boldly proclaimed, "I want to get rid of my bad leg."

For six months, her parents worked with her and the doctors to understand what could be done. They agreed with her and went forward with the amputation. Six months later, the girl saw Mullins at a street fair and went up to tug on her shirt. As Mullins turned to her, the girl hiked up her pant leg to show Mullins her cool new leg.

Beaming during her talk on *The Moth Radio Hour*, Mullins continued the story.

> "[The leg] was pink. And it was tattooed with the characters from High School Musical Three. She was wearing red sequined Mary Janes. And she was proud of it. She was proud of herself. The most marvelous thing was the six-year-old understood something that took me twenty-something years to understand. No matter how we both got there, we both had the discovery that when we celebrate and truly own what it is that makes us different, we're able to find the source of our greatest creative power" (The Moth, 2010).

More than just changing someone's thinking and receiving a good feeling, Mullins' daring to live her best life had empowered that little girl to own who she was. Through having a different way of doing things, Mullins had inspired people to change their life and make it what they really wanted. She did all of this by simply being herself.

As we develop our own process, we sometimes feel isolated from others. We can encourage ourselves by marking the meaning we create in our lives. While we are focusing on ourselves, we have no idea who else will be influenced and what the ripple effect will be. As we go about our purpose, we can also bring meaning to the world around us. Remembering this is crucial when we are making changes in our lives that may feel uncomfortable and tempt us to give up continuing the journey. The key point to remember is the development and application of the process never has to be complete or perfect to matter. It is in bravely being our authentic selves that we make a difference.

> "You don't have to be great to start, but you have to start to be great."
>
> — ZIG ZIGLAR

Looking at someone like Aimee Mullins striking out on her own can be intimidating. The world is set up in a certain way and we are thinking of being different. We have this blank sheet of paper before us. Where do we begin? What direction should I be heading in? What if I get out there and fall off the catwalk?

When I feel the pressure of questions like these, I often can react by trying to take everything on at once, hoping I am covering all the bases. The result is a whirlwind of activity without any progress. I also know people simply freeze in the state of being overwhelmed. To all of us, the best way to begin developing our own process is to simply take one step at a time.

It may seem ridiculous (and I can understand if you suddenly want to throw the book across the room), but a good first step is to develop a process on how we are going to develop a process! How do we know what steps to take? Which one is first? When do we move on to the next step? How will we know we are on our way to making something meaningful?

This first step is to answer these questions and establish a practice to review the answers. It's a way of gauging if you are getting what you want out of the effort. It just needs to be a way of checking in with yourself. It could be journaling; it could be social media; it could be blogging; it could be talking it through with a coach. It comes back to choosing a practice that feels easy for you to do, some way that helps you cut through that chaos and moves you toward what you are trying to accomplish. In a way, it is what you do naturally and making sure you are being true to yourself.

My time with Sarah taught me about this. Sarah is a leader in business strategy and operations, which is corporate business speak for developing processes and solutions for complex problems that touch many kinds of people. While you may not speak corporate, I can tell you Sarah does deliver, so I was curious about how she may be able to help us develop our own process. What were the steps she took? How did she know when she had success? Basically, what was her process?

Before we dove into the specifics, Sarah first told me of her mindset. She said she believed in the value of learning and advised first to explore the means and ways we learn. With that knowledge, she advised,

"Try out ideas, see what sticks, see what works for your personality or temperament, adjust, and then apply. I feel like there's no right or wrong, per se, way to do certain things. Being open to learning and the testing of ideas helps with getting into the core and utilizing the core view more effectively."

I found the concept of a core view interesting. It sounded a great deal like Aimee Mullins' attitude of not being disabled. I asked for Sarah to tell me more. "In my mind, ideas hold certain intrinsic value. Whatever it is, it's an idea and holds its own space. It has its own universe and ecosystem with it. It's up to the ones unfolding or opening up the idea to determine the value of it. If it is interesting enough to pursue and ascribe value to it, then I have given myself permission, the right, and the freedom to jump in and do it."

A list of core guiding principles began to form: open to learning, exploration of ideas, and freedom to express what they mean. When she was in alignment with this core view, it did not matter what role she had or the problem she was solving. She had the confidence she could be herself and accomplish what needed to be done. Stress for her came when she had to separate herself from her core. That was when she was not able to be her true self.

It is because of her core view she cultivated an environment for this at work for herself and her teams. The issue was having many different authentic selves at the table who potentially were in conflict. Sarah often started by defining the objective of the conversation, but with experience she found while a team supported the objectives, each member's understanding of the objective was different depending on their individual viewpoint. This is particularly true when working on strategies, purposes, or processes where the clarity of numbers was not available.

She gave me an example.

"Say we want to work on sustainability and be a sustainable enterprise. I like for us to define what that means. So, what is your definition of sustainability? What is my definition? Can we both articulate that and put that on paper? Can we articulate the objectives or what needs to drive toward sustainability? Let's lay as bare as we can what we think we need to do here and strip it to the very basic [concepts]."

What would that look like? Sarah drove the conversation with questions to pull out the underlying words until she knew everyone got what the concept was. So, for sustainability she may facilitate the conversation this way:

We say we want to be sustainable in the marketplace and we say that means we'll be a leader in the sustainability space. What does that mean? There may be a response that we will be market leaders in driving sustainable actions. What does market leadership mean? We will figure out what the market needs are and then what the customer needs are, and then we'll drive those needs. Are you really being a leader if you're doing that? Do I want to walk in lockstep with the market? Or do I want to go out on a limb and do stuff differently from what market is expecting?

It was a difficult conversation, but then she affirmed, "At the core of it, we all know what we're talking about and we agree this is the basic logic of reference we're supposed to be driving to."

It took a lot of energy and she admitted it would be easier to throw around a lot of high-level corporate speak, but ultimately, Sarah valued the depth of something authentic. So, to protect her energy, Sarah started slowly with something new so she could gauge if it was worth what it would take. She went back to her core view of learning and observing to see what ideas emerged and how they piqued her interest.

As we approach the first step in developing our own process, Sarah's thoughts and methods guide us on what to do and what to expect as we work toward being ourselves. Developing our process takes energy, and we should start slowly to ensure we are investing in ideas that will take us where we want to go. We may think we know where we want to go, but it is good to examine our ideas and ensure we have not made any assumptions about what we want and expect.

ALWAYS GO BACK TO THE CORE

Developing our own process takes energy and that may be difficult to come by when we are burned out. We have talked about how disengaged the workforce is from their jobs and how incorporating reflection into our actions can help us prevent the burnout. We have even talked about ways of combining reflection and action. But what would be helpful to reflect on?

Employers have sought a number of specific ways to motivate employees, and it turns out to not be about money. In 2017, a survey of disengaged employees suggested increasing development would increase performance. Specifically, the top three suggestions were greater clarity from the organization on what needs to be done, more development opportunities, and regular specific feedback (Gaille, 2021).

If we are to motivate ourselves, it can be good to think on how we can provide these three suggestions for ourselves. How can we gain clarity on what needs to be done? What are our development opportunities? How can we get regular and specific feedback?

I would suggest regularly reviewing our core view, what our process means to us, and what we were hoping to become through the process. Since I am working with the moon phases as a timepiece, I perform a review at the beginning of each moon cycle at the new moon. I can compare my efforts in the past cycle to see how successful I have been and what I may need to work on in the next cycle. I have found this to be an essential part of my process.

As 2020 began, my intention was to do more from a place of flow versus forcing myself through tasks. This was my main core view. I knew my best work always came from times when I was "in the zone," and I thought the zone was a subset of being in a place of flow, but I was not completely sure. To find the answer, I knew my effort would need to be supported by self-care and listening to my intuition.

This is how developing my own process became a focus for every cycle throughout the year. I felt my way through the mess for a couple of cycles before I realized I was making decisions only based on my stress level. I wanted to be more proactive in my choices and realized I did not know how to gauge that.

I was working on a separate project on self-care where I was rearranging my bedroom to create a sanctuary. It was a nice-sized space that allowed for a number of different arrangements. I could have chosen to simply move the furniture around and try this or that out. It sounded good, but my gut knew after the second arrangement, I would be exhausted and walk away. Instead, I decided to spend time to understand what a sanctuary meant to me. I heard from my gut this was a place of safety, where I could emerge healthy and refreshed to do my work.

I wasn't sure how that helped with the arrangement of furniture. I dug deeper into what could refresh me. The French doors going out into the deck allowed me to look out at nature. Opening my eyes every morning to that would be refreshing. Having a moment to sit with a cup of tea as my mind and body come to life would let me ease into the day. Both of these thoughts resonated with me and I could then see how the bed needed to sit in the middle of the room and a chair with a night stand would create a nook by the window. To do this, I had to let go of the rules of the bed being against a wall and of a night stand positioned on either side. I then knew what to do and felt free to enjoy the work.

This taught me to spend a moment with my process to understand what it meant to me. I imagined what the results of working my process would be like. I, of course, imagined amazing success and smiles all around. But what does that mean? I wanted to feel confident that I could achieve anything and emerge from it healthy. I wanted to feel solid in who I was. When I interacted with the outside world, I wanted to also know my boundaries so I would be able to agree to work that would fit within my process and walk away from that which would not. I would feel safe and confident and successful.

While it may be an evolving concept, establishing a core view and refining what it means to us will help us evaluate the effectiveness of our effort. We can create a way to stay focused on just being ourselves and run projects through our process. By knowing what needs to be done, seeking out development opportunities, and giving ourselves feedback, we also create a way to keep ourselves motivated. It is in being motivated that we will readily choose to engage with our life.

We then can take a step toward prototyping a process. The first step is to resist the urge to always be busy and to embrace the need for reflection. We can then take the time to establish our core values, look to cycles in nature for what resonates with us, and experiment with ways of applying what we learn. At the end of an experiment, we then go back to the core view, evaluate, and adjust as needed. We will find with each iteration, we gain confidence in who we are and what we are doing. Before you know it, the world turns its head to see you up on a catwalk taking one step at a time, supported by your beautiful hand-carved legs, defying the status quo that it could not be done. You can create your own process that empowers you, brings you energy, and enables you to design a life you love.

Conclusion: A Closing

There are many definitions of success, but the most pervasive aspect of the definition is the idea we are only successful if we are always busy. We take on the assumption that only through constant driving action will we reach the success we desire. We often adopt this definition in large and small ways in our personal and professional lives, such as giving up our weekends to put together that presentation or filling our calendar up so we have no space to prepare for those meetings. In the long term, our efforts are only rewarded with overwhelming stress. We can feel isolated and our vision often narrows to a singular task we choose to work on even harder. As a sense of control eludes us and the results are far less impressive than the effort, we slowly disengage as a means of survival.

> The main question for us is—do we
> have a choice? I say we do.

There are many definitions of success and many other ways of reaching that success. If we can take a moment to look up and widen our view, we can better see how systems within our lives come together, and with that insight, we can see how these can be directed to support our efforts. If we take the time, we will be able to craft a life that not only sees success, but brings us joy as well.

I found myself burned out in 2018 and muddled through the next year trying to regain myself. As I entered 2020, I took a moment to look back at my career and dream of what it might be going forward. I realized that while I had an extensive background in engineering, design, and innovation, I forced each of these disciplines into their own silos because their processes were different. I knew going forward I wanted to bring all of me to the table, and that to me meant I needed my own process of doing things that would allow me to be my best version of myself.

To do this, I wiped the slate clean and started with something completely new, figuring I would add elements of my background as I adapted it. I had always enjoyed being inspired by nature in my design projects, so I looked to nature for processes. I chose to use the moon phases to create a cycle within my life and a timepiece as to when to move to the next step of the process. It was not long when I could see how to insert the elements of my old processes within the cycle.

With that, my projects began to feel more like breathing. There were times where I would receive information, energy, and data and there were times when I would send out creations, ideas, and insights. My victory was threefold. I was not only accomplishing more, but the results of my projects were of higher quality. More importantly, I was enjoying myself throughout the process such that I actually wanted to do more. Lastly, by connecting with nature, I felt connected to something outside of myself and each time I caught a glimpse of the moon, I was reminded I am not alone in this.

The key to everything was shifting my mindset to intentionally instill my actions with moments of reflection. Nature powerfully uses this mindset in everything and innately became my source of inspiration. This allowed me to become a natural reflector and take on a long-term, wider view of success.

Throughout this book, we explored this concept with concrete examples of how people are living their lives and the lessons we can learn from their attempts. Listening to their stories, there is hope we can take the best of their offerings and apply them to our own lives to become more reflective in our actions.

The world celebrates being busy so much so that there is a cult of action pressuring each and every one of us to conform to its ideology. If we attempt to flee the overwork, we are seen as weak and disloyal. As a collective, we can change this by realistically viewing what it takes to be successful in this system. We can see the leaders of this cult are not superheroes who defy reality, but flawed humans who are making choices about their lives. If we can see them in this realistic light, we can see ourselves as human and move to act in such a way that embraces and celebrates who we are as we choose how to engage with the system.

Reflection is a foreign concept in this modern world, but it is needed if we are to hear from our intuition on the quality of our decisions. Is what we are working on good? Are we happy with the results? If we are not well versed in our intuition's language, then we may need to slow down to make space to hear it. Those of us in the Western world struggle to slow down because we view time as linear, finite, and always slipping through our fingers. There is a constant sense of loss that causes us to grasp for whatever we can get a hold of, even when we don't want it. Alternatively, other cultures see time moving in great circles that are always refreshing. If we adopt a view of time moving in a cycle, we can see a time of reflection not as failure, but as opportunity to improve our lives by developing a process that includes reflection.

A healthy process requires both reflection and action. Professions like nursing, teaching, sports and even comedy achieve bringing reflection and action together in unique and different ways. These examples can inspire us on how to create our own methods, to adopt new mindsets and to integrate technologies to make the process more impactful. Different examples show us there are a number of options available to us and having options prompts us to be flexible in how we apply methods to our processes. The key is to try and see what fits well, while keeping ourselves open to adjustments for what we learn along the way.

The objective is to develop a process that is totally ours. Each one of us in unique with our own set of talents, skills, temperaments, and experiences. There is no reason to force ourselves into someone else's process. To enjoy the success we long for, our process needs to be an authentic extension of who we are and refined as we change. This can mean we do use someone else's process, particularly those who come from our families or a lifelong career, but we make an intentional choice to use it because it is to our benefit, not because it is the status quo.

Before we even start, we need a paradigm shift away from the cult of action. This requires taking a moment to reflect on how the cult of action influences us, what we would be giving up if we walked away, and what the benefits would be if we made changes. We can then knowingly make the choice to shift and gain the benefit of directing how the shift happens. We are then motivated to examine our own preconceived notions and choose what needs to be changed, eliminated, or upgraded. This takes intentional times of honest reflection since these notions have been cultivated from a million microscopic things in our lives, and changing them can feel like someone has died. It is advisable then to let all the feelings, information, and thoughts settle to give us clarity before moving to action. Reacting to being overwhelmed by driving to action is part of the cult of action. We are in charge of how this moves forward. We need to mentally shift to be able to develop a process that supports us and does not rule us.

With this new mindset, we are open to seeing new sources of inspiration. Nature has many options on how to develop processes, particularly those combining reflection and action to achieve greater things in the long term. The key is to observe the various options and reflect how one or more can apply to our lives. Some of nature's processes will simply require watching or listening, but some will require more consideration to reveal each new layer. Despite all the differences, there are some parallels between processes within nature, and these commonalities utilize a rhythm or cycle that repeats over and over. We can tap into these similarities to get started applying nature's teachings.

As we move to creating our own process, we will find this takes significant energy because change can be uncomfortable. To counteract the discomfort, we should make this fun and know we are just playing with some ideas. To conserve energy, though, it helps to make sure we are choosing wisely. Some ideas are worth investing in more than others. When we take the time to know and define where we are and where we'd like to go, we have established the criteria on what is a good idea and what is not. We have taken the time to articulate what our intuition has been trying to tell us, and with the definition of what we want, the logical mind is able to readily get on board and pull together plans. Knowing ourselves can give us a core view to always go back to as a litmus test to check how well we are developing and working our process.

As I went back to my core view over and over, I found it interesting how it changed yet remained the same as I made this journey of writing about developing processes. I started with a process—my process—and how I had followed the moon cycles. I even felt I had something unique by inserting elements of the design process within that cycle. For me, it resonated and felt authentic. As I wrote and began to share what it was about, people would present other processes to me and compare the two. Sometimes, the image of the two side by side was complementary and beautiful; other times it was jarring and abrasive. There was no right or wrong; the differences were completely valid. While I had found what worked for me, it became clear writing a book with only my process would not have been as helpful to anyone picking up this book.

So, my journey expanded into exploring other processes and finding I also expanded my definition of "nature" from what was going on outside of my window to include what was also stirring inside of me. Reflection was a core feature of my process, and with the exploration inside, authenticity and tendencies became core features as well. For myself, I started looking not only for how to be successful, but how to set myself up well for achieving that success. I could then interact with the world's processes and be true to myself by orbiting it versus blindly submitting to it.

Ultimately, I wrote this book to help people think differently about how things are accomplished and to show there are possibilities beyond what we have been taught and told. There is something besides burnout for us. New possibilities can lead to changed lives, even if it is only in giving ourselves permission. If we can see we are empowered, then we can appreciate the chance we have to make our own choices; we can consider what we want to protect, to change, and to release from our lives; and we learn we are people in the middle of an amazing journey.

My hope is by reading this book, you will see you are not alone in the thought there must be a better way. My greater hope is after reading this, you will develop your own process that includes reflection to make your actions far more extraordinary and to connect all you do to your best self. As you take on this adventure, a number of questions will likely arise. Where do I begin? Should I mimic someone else's process or start with a blank slate? How would this work for me? Reflection is the conduit that allows you to hear the answers to any questions. We are each unique and constantly changing. While you may seek advice from others, only you can know what is best for you. Using reflection in your process is crucial to preserving your authentic self. This also means while parts of your process may be similar to others, there will be parts that are uniquely your own. Others will notice the difference and want to understand what you are doing. That's when you know you have made it and have the chance to add your own story of developing processes.

So now, it's time for you to begin your journey from being burnt out to designing a life that engages you. I beg you to not simply put this book down and go back to busyness. Take a moment and reflect on what brings you joy and what does not. Listen to your intuition for what is good and let your logic figure out how to bring more of that good into your life. Find ways to regularly check in because as you continue the journey, there will be times when you are confused or struggling. There will be times when this doesn't feel like the effort is getting anywhere and you will want to give up. Those are the times when you will be grateful you have learned your body's language and you will be able to make an impactful decision.

Throughout my journey of developing my process and even of writing this book, I have leaned on the advice I have been given so many times. "Jennifer, trust the process." Trust takes time to develop and it is our choice where to place our trust. We can decide to trust someone else's process. We can opt to trust our own process. What I learned is when I reflect, I come to know what is best for me. When we devote ourselves to reflection, we gain greater clarity where to place our trust so our trust has the chance to grow. Is that not where burnout comes from—blindly trusting someone else's process and waking up to find we misplaced our trust?

When you take on the investment of developing your own process, you are taking active steps in learning how to trust yourself, and you are worthy of it.

Acknowledgments

I would like to thank all those who have made this book possible. I never in my wildest dreams had being an author on my bucket list and yet, as I began, there have been so many who have encouraged and walked the journey with me.

It certainly starts with all who were open to being interviewed. This includes Dr. Andres Tellez, Dr. Byungsoo Kim, Dr. Hongyang Liu, Mohit Kamat, Stacy Levy, Dr. Dnyanada Satam, Dr. Engin Kapkin, Elizabeth, Catalina Salamanca, and Sarah Bassey. It takes great patience to put yourself in another's hands, particularly when it is not just a conversation over coffee but will be put into print. It was a humbling experience to witness their vulnerability and have their trust.

I also greatly appreciate Whitney Jones, my development editor, who patiently listened to all my thoughts, feelings, and words through creating the manuscript. She patiently taught me how to sort through those for myself and even more on how to get the words on the page. It has often been her faith in me that kept me going.

My time with Whitney was made possible by Eric Koester and the Creator Institute, where I was given the opportunity to start this adventure. It was not only Eric's vision to make book writing open to so many, but his time coaching me that broadened the scope of my book to something more readers will enjoy.

A number of people read portions of the book while it was in revisions and I am grateful for their words, honesty, and encouragement. Thank you again, Jeanette Battista-Lucas, Jeffrey Philips, Dr. Amanda Mills, Kim McEachron, Dr. Sharon Joines, Dr. Hongyang Liu, Sean Mitton, Sharon Justice, Michelle Grainger, Kaan Gunes, Melissa Pasquinelli, and Carlo Mahouz. There were also three who took the time to go through every word: Jeff Stikeleather, Sherry Davis, and Dr. Charlie Gooding. Thank you all for your perseverance and dedication. Having your insights made this work better than it ever could have been.

Last but not least, there was an army of people who made the production of the book possible. Thank you to all those with New Degree Press who made this a reality, but especially thank you to all of those who believed in me enough to fund my work. Those who contributed were Jeff and Jane Stikeleather, Sharon Joines, Scott Clear, Gary J. Hayes, Mary McBride, Michael A. Cafasso, Tamie Wells, Timothy Peret, Jonathan Stephens, Marc Edlein, Stephen B. Leonard, Daniel Abramowicz, Nate Miranda, Michael A. Swartz, Kevin Mitchell, Tsailu Liu, Greg McCann, William Prisbrey, Michelle Grainger, Amanda Myers, Melissa Pasquinelli, Holli Alexander, Wade Ingram, Elizabeth King, Jaclyn Moxham, Daniel McGurrin, Connie Lippert, Kyle Kramer, Jon Paul Rust,

Jeffrey Phillips, Engin Kapkin, Trent Bolling, Sean Mitton, Sally and Bruce Ainslie, Debra Lucenti, Sumita Ranganathan, Melvin Melchor, Wesley Hare, Charles Gooding, Nate Jones, Jos de Wit, Thomas Henning, Sharon Justice, Haig Khachatoorian, Kathleen Davis, Braden Li, Kaan Gunes, Brian Himelright, Michael Dickey, Paul B. Germeraad, Andres Tellez, Makana Dumlao, Danielle Kaynor, Warren Ginn, Kim E. McEachron, George Wofford, Alan Parr, Joyce Cole, Cliff Kendrick , Eric Pike, Carlo Mahfouz, Nancy Eichstadt, Adam Kaynan, Owen Foster, David Culton, Danielle Goslen, Scott Gainer, Sol Wilder, Matthew Dudas, David Norman, Alan Lee, Tom Keegan, Kelly Umstead, David Mattison, John K. Caruso, Patricia Streeper, Sylvester Taylor, Jane Nsunwara, Jeffrey Chen, Mingyu Liu, Peter Johnson, David Eidson, Courtney Lee, Mohit Kamat, Sachin Sakhalkar, Keith Gausmann, Sherry Davis, Catalina Salamanca, Eric Koester, Dnyanada Satam, Zoe Rosenberg, Karen E O'Connell, Bailey Knight, Kayla Geer, Casey Kivett, Jane Casteline, Gaylon H. White, Denny Stilwell, Chris Teague, Byungsoo Kim, Hongyang Liu, Ben Gillespie , Kevin Grevemberg, Kyrsten Rudock, Carly Kvietok, Megan Helton, Hannah Rich, Will Marrs, Tracy Manning, Alek Walker, Jessica Coates, Dawn Mason, Carol Perkins, Joe Mahaffey, Charity Kirk, Raj Bhakta, Paul Barnes, and Chef Avenue.

Appendix

___

INTRODUCTION

Arylo, Christine. "Embrace your power to create the world you want to live in." Accessed March 10, 2021. https://christinearylo.com/.

Casarella, Jennifer. "Causes of Stress." WebMD. March 09, 2020. https://www.webmd.com/balance/guide/causes-of-stress.

CBS Interactive, Inc. "Why 'side hustles' are on the rise." October 8, 2019. https://www.cbsnews.com/news/side-hustle-jobs-on-the-rise-behind-the-popularity/.

Chelala, Cesar. "The secret to Lionel Messi's soccer success." *The Japan Times*, June 20, 2015. https://www.japantimes.co.jp/opinion/2015/06/20/commentary/world-commentary/secret-lionel-messis-soccer-success/#:~:text=%E2%80%9CThe%20secret%2C%E2%80%9D%20he%20says,him%20not%20to%20be%20caught.%E2%80%9D.

Covert, Bryce. "The American Work Ethic." *Longreads*, April 8, 2019. https://longreads.com/2019/04/08/the-american-worth-ethic/.

FC Barcelona. "Lionel Messi." Accessed March 10, 2021. https://www.fcbarcelona.com/en/football/first-team/players/4974/lionel-messi.

Fearless Motivation. "15 Powerful Lionel Messi Quotes to Help You Achieve Your Dreams." Accessed March 10, 2021. https://www.fearlessmotivation.com/2017/03/11/15-powerful-lionel-messi-quotes/.

Fyucha, John. "17 best Lionel Messi Quotes on Football, Life and Success." *John Fyucha (blog)*, March 17, 2019. https://www.john-fyucha.com/2019/03/17-best-lionel-messi-quotes-on-football.html.

Nielsen, Chad. "What I do is play soccer." *ESPN The Magazine*, May 25, 2009. https://www.espn.com/espn/news/story?id=4205057.

Oppong, Thomas. "How to practice long term thinking when you can barely see past tomorrow." *Medium*, May 12, 2020. https://medium.com/personal-growth/how-to-practice-long-term-thinking-when-you-can-barely-see-past-tomorrow-a5f-68540aa8a.

Quoidbach, Jordi, Daniel T. Gilbert, and Timothy D. WIlson, "The End of History Illusion." *Science*, 309, no. 6115 (January 04, 2013): 96-98. https://science.sciencemag.org/content/339/6115/96. https://wjh-www.harvard.edu/~dtg/Quoidbach%20et%20al%202013.pdf.

Spencer, Dr. Ezzie. "re.love." Accessed March 10, 2021. https://www.ezziespencer.com/.

Soccer Training Info. "Lionel Messi's Change of Pace." June 26, 2019. https://soccer-training-info.com/messi_change_of_pace/.

Soleil, Gina. "Workplace Stress: The Health Epidemic of the 21st Century." *The Huffington Post,* January 7, 2016. https://www.huffpost.com/entry/workplace-stress-the-heal_b_8923678.

World Health Organization. "Burn-out an 'occupational phenomenon': International Classification of Diseases." Accessed March 10, 2021. https://www.who.int/news/item/28-05-2019-burn-out-an-occupational-phenomenon-international-classification-of-diseases.

World Health Organization. "Mental health in the workplace." Accessed March 10, 2021. https://www.who.int/teams/mental-health-and-substance-use/mental-health-in-the-workplace.

CHAPTER ONE: THE CULT OF ACTION

"Criticism of Black Leaders," *The New York Times,* November 20, 1984, Section A, Page 14. https://www.nytimes.com/1984/11/20/us/criticism-of-black-leaders.html.

Don Henley. "Don Henley – The Garden of Allah." January 9, 2021. Video, 7:12. https://www.youtube.com/watch?v=DlWqxTpsrnk

Frey, Carl Benedikt, and Michael A. Osborne. "The Future of Employment: How Susceptible are Jobs to Computerisation?"

Technological Forecasting and Social Change 114, no. C (January 2017): 254-280. https://doi.org/10.1016/j.techfore.2016.08.019.

Hastings Museum of Natural and Cultural History. "The History of Kool-Aid." Accessed March 11. 2021. https://web.archive. org/web/20080615160059/http://www.hastingsmuseum.org/ koolaid/kahistory.htm.

Higgins, Chris. "Stop Saying 'Drink the Kool-Aid'." *The Atlantic*, November 8, 2012. https://www.theatlantic.com/health/ archive/2012/11/stop-saying-drink-the-kool-aid/264957/.

Kelly, Martin. "Historical Significance of the Cotton Gin." ThoughtCo. July 09, 2019. https://www.thoughtco.com/the- cotton-gin-in-american-history-104722.

Menke, S.M. "Oracle: 'Drink the Kool-Aid' for e-success." *GCN*, 1105 Media, April 27, 2001. https://gcn.com/Articles/2001/04/27/ Oracle-Drink-the-KoolAid-for-esuccess.aspx.

Meyer, Holly. "What makes a cult a cult?" *Tennessean*, September 15, 2016. https://www.tennessean.com/story/news/reli- gion/2016/09/15/what-makes-cult-cult/90377532/.

Moore, Rebecca. "Drinking the Kool Aid: The Cultural Transfor- mation of a Tragedy." *Alternative Considerations of Jonestown & Peoples Temple*, March 11, 2013. https://jonestown.sdsu. edu/?page_id=16584.

National Park Service. "The Legend of John Henry: Talcott, WV." Accessed March 11, 2021. https://www.nps.gov/neri/planyour- visit/the-legend-of-john-henry-talcott-wv.htm.

Netflix. "The Queen's Gambit." Accessed May 24, 2021. https://www.netflix.com/title/80234304.

Perkins Products Company. "Easy to Make Kool-Aid Treats!" Accessed March 11, 2021. https://www.flickr.com/photos/curly-wurly/7012903347/in/photostream.

Pfeffer, Jeffrey. *Leadership BS: Fixing Workplaces and Careers One Truth at a Time*. United States: Harper Business, 2015.

Robot Workforce. "IBM's Watson on Jeopardy!" March 31, 2013. Video, 2:21. https://www.youtube.com/watch?v=Sp4q6oBsHoY.

Talks at Google. "Leadership BS | Jeffrey Pfeffer | Talks at Google." November 9, 2015. Video, 52:55. https://www.youtube.com/watch?v=pFXcqSUi3EI.

TED. "Tim Leberecht – TEDSummit: 4 ways to build a human company in the age of machines." Uploaded November 2, 2016. Accessed June 3, 2021. https://www.ted.com/talks/tim_leberecht_4_ways_to_build_a_human_company_in_the_age_of_machines?language=en.

UNSW Business School, "Trouble at work: Jeffrey Pfeffer on fixing leadership failure – BusinessThink," October 14, 2014, Video, 10:53. https://www.youtube.com/watch?v=JfJezKekY5g&feature=emb_logo.

Weiner, Yitzi. "Social Impact Heroes: 'How Yael Cohen Braun & Julie Greenbaum are helping to change the way people talk about cancer and help provide equitable access to support.' *Authority Magazine*, November 19, 2019. https://medium.com/authority-magazine/social-impact-heroes-how-yael-cohen-braun-ju-lie-greenbaum-are-helping-to-change-the-way-d0e47c158201.

Westfall, Chris. "Leadership Development Is A $366 Billion Industry: Here's Why Most Programs Don't Work." *Forbes*, June 20, 2019. https://www.forbes.com/sites/chriswestfall/2019/06/20/leadership-development-why-most-programs-dont-work/?sh=-4242bec61de4.

Wolfe, Tom. *The Electric Kool-Aid Acid Test.* New York: Bantam Books, 1999.

CHAPTER TWO: NATURAL REFLECTION

Arylo, Christine. "Embrace your power to create the world you want to live in." Accessed March 10, 2021. https://christinea-rylo.com.

Baechu Kimchi. "What is Kimchi? A Brief Science of Lacto-Fermentation." Accessed March 12, 2021. https://baechukimchi.ca/kimchi-and-lacto-fermentation/.

Baird, Benjamin, Jonathan Smallwood, Michael D. Mrazek, Julia W. Y. Kam, Michael S. Franklin, and Jonathan W. Schooler. "Inspired by Distraction: Mind Wandering Facilitates Creative Incubation." *Psychological Science* 23, no. 10 (October 2012): 1117–22. https://doi.org/10.1177/0956797612446024.

British Design Council, "Eleven Lessons: Managing Design in Eleven Global Companies." November 5, 2007. https://www.

designcouncil.org.uk/sites/default/files/asset/document/ElevenLessons_DeskResearchReport_o.pdf.

CelloBello. "Yo-Yo Ma interview: On Practicing." October 23, 2017. Video, 5:45. https://www.youtube.com/watch?v=qsnrWNYMFvI.

Chin, Mei. "The Art of Kimchi." *Saveur*, October 14, 2009. https://www.saveur.com/article/Kitchen/The-Art-of-Kimchi/.

Dijksterhuis, Ap, Maarten W. Bos, Loran F. Nordgren, and Rick B. Van Baaren. "On Making the Right Choice: The Deliberation-Without-Attention Effect." *Science* 311, no. 5763 (February 17, 2006): 1005-7. https://doi.org/10.1126/science.1121629.

Ericcson, K. Anders, Ralf Th. Krampe, and Clemens Tesch-Romer. "The Role of Deliberate Practice in the Acquisition of Expert Performance." *Psychological Review* 100, no. 3 (1993): 363-406. https://doi.org/10.1098/rsos.190327.

Ford, Holly. "Kimchi or Kimchee, mastering the art of Kimchee vol 3." Beyond Kimchee: Real Korean Food and Beyond. Accessed March 12, 2021. https://www.beyondkimchee.com/cabbage-kimchi-or-kimchee-part-3/.

Goleman, Daniel. *Emotional intelligence: why it can matter more than IQ.* New York: Bantam Books, 1995.

Honoré, Carl. "In Praise of Slowness." TED Ideas worth spreading. Recorded July 2005. Accessed March 12, 2021. https://www.ted.com/talks/carl_honore_in_praise_of_slowness?referrer=playlist-slow_down_enjoy_life#t-6365.

Immordino-Yang, Mary Helen, Joanna A. Christodoulou, and Vanessa Singh. "Rest Is Not Idleness: Implications of the Brain's Default Mode for Human Development and Education." *Perspectives on Psychological Science* 7, no. 4 (July 2012): 352–64. https://doi.org/10.1177/1745691612447308.

Middleton, Scott. 2019. "Design Process: 3 Most Popular Product Design Processes & When To Use Them." Agile Insider. 2019. https://medium.com/agileinsider/3-product-design-processes-and-when-to-use-them-2c6552522637.

Moore, Eric. "Unpacking Yo-Yo Ma's practice routine – part 1 of 2." Cello Loft. Accessed March 12, 2021. https://www.celloloft.com/blog/practice-like-yo-yo-ma-1.

Pollen, Michael. *Cooked: A Natural History of Transformation.* New York: The Penguin Press, 2013.

Soencer, Dr. Ezzie. "re.love." Accessed March 10, 2021. https://www.ezziespencer.com.

TEDx Talks. "5 Steps to designing the life you want | Bill Burnett | TEDxStanford." May 19, 2017. Video, 25:20. https://www.youtube.com/watch?v=SemHhon19LA.

CHAPTER THREE: CAN ACTION AND REFLECTION COEXIST?

Bernardini, Gabrielle. "Is the Long-Running Improv Comedy Series 'Whose Line Is It Anyway?' Rehearsed?" *Distractify.*

August 19, 2019. https://www.distractify.com/p/is-whose-line-is-it-anyway-rehearsed.

Cole, Jordana. "I've Got Your Back: Utilizing Improv as a Tool to Enhance Workplace Relationships." Master of Applied Positive Psychology (MAPP) Capstone Projects. University of Pennsylvannia, August 1, 2016.

Dailymotion. "Whose Line Is It Anyway- – S4 E 8 – Kathy Greenwood." Accessed June 23, 2021. https://www.dailymotion.com/video/x5188ih.

Edwards, Allan. "Reflective Practice in Sport Management." *Sport Management Review 2*, no. 1 (1999): 67-81. https://doi.org/10.1016/S1441-3523(99)70090-2.

Fandom Whose Line is It Anyway Wiki. "Living Scenery." Accessed June 23, 2021. https://whoselineisitanyway.fandom.com/wiki/Living_Scenery.

Kevin Durham. "Colin Mochrie Interview – Star of Whose Line – How to Do Improvisational Comedy (Improv Comedy Tips)." January 4, 2021. Video, 2:43. https://www.youtube.com/watch?v=3LzZhvKrG2s.

La Trobe University. "What is reflective practice?" Accessed March 15, 2021. https://latrobe.libguides.com/reflectivepractice/introduction.

Larkin, Bob. "50 Amazing Jokes from Comedy Legends." *Best Life Online.* April 3, 2018. https://bestlifeonline.com/50-amazing-jokes-from-comedy-legends/.

Lee, Hulbert. "How to Tell a Funny Joke." *LifeHack.* Accessed May 6, 2021. https://www.lifehack.org/articles/communication/how-to-tell-a-funny-joke.html.

Mayo Clinic. "Stress Management." Accessed May 6, 2021. https://www.mayoclinic.org/healthy-lifestyle/stress-management/in-depth/stress-relief/art-20044456.

Olteanu, Constanta. "Reflection-for-action and the choice or design of examples in the teaching of mathematics." *Mathematics Education Research* Journal 29, (2017): ** 349–367. https://doi.org/10.1007/s13394-017-0211-9.

Rotten Tomatoes. "Kathy Greenwood (Episode 8) Whose Line Is It Anyway? Season 4." Accessed June 23, 2021. https://www.rottentomatoes.com/tv/whose_line_is_it_anyway_us_/s04/e08.

Rūmī, Jalāl al-Dīn 1207-1273 and Coleman Barks. *"The Essential Rumi."* San Francisco, CA: Harper, 1996.

Stearns-Pfeiffer, Amanda. "Using Standards as an Opportunity for Teacher Reflection Revisting the 'Best Practices' Debate." *Language Arts Journal of Michigan* 27, no. 1 (2011): 13-15. https://doi.org/10.9707/2168-149X.1828.

Wright, Geoff. "Improving Teacher Performance Using an Enhanced Digital Video Reflection Technique." *Learning and Instruction in the Digital Age,* ed. J. Michael Spector, et al. 175-190. Boston: Springer-Verlag, 2010. 175-190.

CHAPTER FOUR: DEVELOPING YOUR OWN PROCESS

C-Span. "Highest Duty." November 9, 2010. Video, 4:03. https://www.c-span.org/video/?296623-18/highest-duty.

Gino, *Francesca. Rebel Talent: Why It Pays to Break the Rules at Work and in Life.* New York: Dey Street Books, 2018.

Inc. "Captain Sully's Minute-by-Minute Description of The Miracle on The Hudson | Inc." March 6, 2009. Video, 12:22. https://www.youtube.com/watch?v=w6EblErBJqw.

MacKenzie, Gordon. *Orbiting the Giant Hairball: A Corporate Fool's Guide to Surviving with Grace.* New York: Viking, 1998.

Montgomery, William T. and Shannon L. Laegeler. "An Analysis of the Army's Formal Bureaucracy and the Impact on Acquisition Cycles." Joint Applied Project. Naval Postgraduate School, September 2017. https://apps.dtic.mil/dtic/tr/fulltext/u2/1046889.pdf.

National Transportation Safety Board. "Loss of Thrust in Both Engines After Encountering a Flock of Birds and Subsequent Ditching on the Hudson River US Airways Flight 1549 Airbus A320-214, N106US Weehawken, New Jersey." Accident Reports NTSB/AAR-10/03 and PB2010-910403. January 15, 2009. Accessed March 16, 2021. https://www.ntsb.gov/investigations/AccidentReports/Reports/AAR1003.pdf.

Roulo, Claudette. "DoD Seeks to Cut Red Tape, Bureaucracy, Officials Say." *DoD News, US Department of Defense.* November

15, 2014. https://www.defense.gov/Explore/News/Article/Article/603654/dod-seeks-to-cut-red-tape-bureaucracy-officials-say/.

Savani, Krishna, Michael W. Norris and N. V. R. Naidu, "Deference in Indians' Decision Making: Introjected Goals or Injunctive Norms?" *Journal of Personality and Social Psychology* 102, no. 4 (December 2011): 685-99. https://doi.apa.org/doiLanding?-doi=10.1037%2Fa0026415.

Sparknotes. 'What is Bureaucracy?" Accessed, March 16, 2021. https://www.sparknotes.com/us-government-and-politics/american-government/the-bureaucracy/section1/

Sullenberger, Chesley and Jeffrey Zaslaw. *Highest Duty: My Search for What Really Matters.* New York: HarperCollins, 2009.

Talks at Google. "Rebel Talent: Why it Pays to Break the Rules | Professor Gino | Talks at Google." November 8, 2018. Video, 52:11. https://www.youtube.com/watch?v=GQywxCy-Dz8.

Todd, Sarah. "The Steve Jobs speech that made Silicon Valley obsessed with pirates." *Quartz*, October 22, 2019. https://qz.com/1719898/steve-jobs-speech-that-made-silicon-valley-obsessed-with-pirates/.

CHAPTER FIVE: SHIFT THE MINDSET

Ambardekar, MD, Nayana. "Vertigo." *WebMD.* December 17, 2020. https://www.webmd.com/brain/vertigo-symptoms-causes-treatment#1.

Chen, James. "Industrial Revolution." *Investopedia*. February 25, 2021. https://www.investopedia.com/terms/i/industrial-revolution.asp.

Clark, Brian. "7 of the Biggest Problems with the Music Industry?" *Musician Wave*. March 5, 2021. https://www.musicianwave.com/biggest-problems-with-the-music-industry/.

Fauquier ENT. "Epley Maneuver to Treat BPPV Vertigo." September 27, 2014. Video, 2:25. https://www.youtube.com/watch?v=9SLm76jQg3g&vl=en.

Gaur, Sushil, et al. "Efficacy of Epley's Maneuver in Treating BPPV Patients: A Prospective Observational Study." Int J Otolaryngol. 2015, (2015): 487160. https://doi.org/10.1155/2015/487160.

Google Dictionary. "ambiguity." Accessed March 18, 2021. https://www.google.com/search?q=ambiguity&rlz=1C5CHFA_enUS803US803&oq=ambiguity&aqs=chrome.69i57j69i-59j0i395i433l3j0i395l3.1641j1j15&sourceid=chrome&ie=UTF-8.

Huey, Steve. "Sheryl Crow Biography." AllMusic. Accessed March 18, 2021. https://www.allmusic.com/artist/sheryl-crow-mn0000080780.

Kelly, Mary Louise, Noah Caldwell and Sarah Handel. "Sheryl Crow Says 'Threads' Is Her Last Album. And She's OK with That." *NPR Music Interviews*. August 29, 2019. https://www.npr.org/2019/08/29/755079071/sheryl-crow-says-threads-is-her-last-album-and-she-s-ok-with-that.

Kenton, Will. "Paradigm Shift." *Investopedia*. June 27, 2019. https://www.investopedia.com/terms/p/paradigm-shift.asp.

Larratt, Stephanie. "'It's scary to be vulnerable': Celebrities talk conquering fear and finding success." *Today*. March 24, 2020. https://www.today.com/tmrw/overcoming-fear-celebs-share-inspiring-stories-about-overcoming-fear-t173976.

Rodman, Sarah. "Sheryl Crow shares the stories and secrets behind her final full-length album, Threads." *Entertainment Weekly*. September 4, 2019. https://ew.com/music/2019/09/04/sheryl-crow-breaks-down-her-final-album-threads/.

Sheryl Crow. "Sheryl Crow." Accessed March 18, 2021. https://sherylcrow.com/sheryl-crow/.

Songfacts. "Everyday Is A Winding Road." Accessed March 18, 2021. https://www.songfacts.com/facts/sheryl-crow/everyday-is-a-winding-road.

Wiktionary. "gurbet." Accessed March 18, 2021. https://en.wiktionary.org/wiki/gurbet.

CHAPTER SIX: BE INSPIRED BY NATURE

Boston University School of Medicine. "Repeated head impacts associated with later-life depression symptoms, worse cognitive function." *ScienceDaily*. Accessed March 18, 2021. www.sciencedaily.com/releases/2020/06/200626161159.htm (http://www.sciencedaily.com/releases/2020/06/200626161159.htm).

Eurich, Tasha. *Insight: Why We're Not as Self-aware as We Think, and how Seeing Ourselves Clearly Helps Us Succeed at Work and in Life*. United States: Crown Business, 2017.

Google Dictionary. "nature." accessed March 19, 2021. https://tinyurl.com/5nfbhf63.

Grant, Amy. "Apple Chilling Info: How Many Chill Hours Do Apples Need." Gardening Know How. July 27, 2020. https://www.gardeningknowhow.com/edible/fruits/apples/chill-hours-for-apple-trees.htm#.

Himmel, David. "Chicago Brain Doc Goes Hollywood." *Chicago Health*. January 26, 2016. https://chicagohealthonline.com/chicago-brain-doc-goes-hollywood/.

Kauflin, Jeff. "Only 15% Of People Are Self-Aware — Here's How to Change." *Forbes*. May 10, 2017. https://www.forbes.com/sites/jeffkauflin/2017/05/10/only-15-of-people-are-self-aware-heres-how-to-change/?sh=24295cda2b8c.

Live Science. "How Roots Know Where to Grow." Accessed March 19, 2021. https://www.livescience.com/2331-roots-grow.html.

NorthShore University HealthSystem. "Julian E. Bales, M.D." Accessed March 19, 2021. https://www.northshore.org/apps/findadoctor/physicians/julian-e.-bailes.

Q30 Innovations, "The Brain Injury Epidemic." Accessed March 19, 2021. https://q30innovations.com/.

Roberts, Nicole F. "Bird Brains: Why Don't Woodpeckers Get Concussions?" *Forbes*. January 6, 2016. https://www.forbes.com/sites/nicolefisher/2016/01/06/bird-brains-why-dont-woodpeckers-get-concussions/?sh=66dbe0544256.

SoftSchools. "Woodpecker Facts." Accessed March 19, 2021. https://www.softschools.com/facts/animals/woodpecker_facts/323/.

Soniak, Matt. "Why Don't Woodpeckers Get Brain Damage?" *Mental Floss*. November 24, 2014. https://www.mentalfloss.com/article/30731/why-dont-woodpeckers-get-brain-damage.

Swaminathan, Nikhil. "Our Brains on Marketing: Scans Show Why We Like New Things." *Scientific American*. June 26, 2008. https://www.scientificamerican.com/article/our-brains-on-marketing-s/.

TH Tree Services. "Trees Through the Seasons." Accessed March 19, 2021. https://thtreeservices.co.uk/trees-through-the-seasons/.

Turner, Ryan C., et al., "Effect of slosh mitigation on histologic markers of traumatic brain injury: laboratory investigation." *J Neurosurg* 117, no. 6 (Dec 2012): 1110-18. https://doi.org/10.3171/2012.8.JNS12358.

Viviano, JoAnne. "Concussion prevention: Can woodpecker-inspired collar reduce brain injuries in athletes, service members?" *The Columbus Dispatch*. December 18, 2017. https://www.dispatch.com/news/20171218/concussion-prevention-can-woodpecker-inspired-collar-reduce-brain-injuries-in-athletes-service-members.

CHAPTER SEVEN: LAYER UPON LAYER

Clark, Donald. "Gem Formation: How are Gemstones Created?" International Gem Society. Accessed May 11, 2021. https://www.gemsociety.org/article/gem-formation/#:~:text=Gems%20Formed%20in%20othe%20Earth's%20Mantle,-Our%20knowledge%20of.

Gaboury, Bernie. "World's Most Famous Gemstones." Travel Channel. Accessed May 11, 2021. travelchannel.com/interests/arts-and-culture/photos/worlds-most-famous-gemstones?page=11 (http://travelchannel.com/interests/arts-and-culture/photos/worlds-most-famous-gemstones?page=11).

Geiger, Beth. "Explainer: Earth — layer by layer." *ScienceNewsforStudent.*, November 11, 2019. https://www.sciencenewsforstudents.org/article/explainer-earth-layer-layer#:~:text=Starting%20at%20othe%20center%2C%20Earth,explored%20othese%20olayers%20oin%20operson.

Gemfields. 2021a. "Sustainability." Accessed May 11, 2021. https://gemfields.com/sustainability/.

Gemfields. 2021b. "Kagem." Accessed May 11, 2021. https://gemfields.com/our-mines-assets/kagem/.

Gemfields. 2021c. "Our Assets in Detail." Accessed May 11, 2021. https://gemfields.com/our-mines-assets/our-assets-in-detail/.

Hammond, Martin, Marcus Aurelius et. al. Meditations. New Delhi: Digital Fire, 2019.

Lindy Institute for Urban Innovation. "Art@Bartrams." Accessed May 12, 2021. https://issuu.com/lindyinstituteforurbaninnov/docs/art-at-bartrams_dig-spreads.

Mural Arts Philadelphia 2021a. "About." Accessed May 12, 2021. https://www.muralarts.org/about/.

Mural Arts Philadelphia 2021b. "Art@Bartram's." Accessed May 12, 2021. https://www.muralarts.org/artworks/artbartrams/.

Pardieu, Vincent. "Update on emerald mining at Kagem, Zambia," *Gems and Gemology,* 47, no. 1 (Spring 2011): 63-65.

Somarin, Ali. "Where Did Those Gemstones Come From?" *ThermoFisher Scientific Blog,* March 20, 2014. https://www.thermofisher.com/blog/mining/where-did-those-gemstones-come-from/#:~:text=How%20Are%20Gemstones%20Found%3F,is%20a%20very%20different%20process.

Stacy Levy. 2021a. "Artist's Statement." Accessed May 12, 2021. https://www.stacylevy.com/statement.

Stacy Levy. 2021b. "Tampa Wind." Accessed May 12, 2021. https://www.stacylevy.com/tampa-wind.

Stacy Levy. 2021c. "Rose Level." Accessed May 12, 2021. https://www.stacylevy.com/rose-level.

stacylevyART. "Tide Field Art on the Schuylkill River." August 8, 2018. Video, 3:32. https://www.youtube.com/watch?v=6q-s0XXKN70.

Zink, Sharon. "97% of Writers Never Finish Their Novels: Here's Why." SharonZink. Accessed May 11, 2021. http://sharonzink. com/writing-tips/97-of-writers-never-finish-their-novels-her- es-why/.

CHAPTER EIGHT: FINDING PATTERNS IN NATURE

AZ Quotes. "Henry David Thoreau, 'It is not enough to be busy'." Accessed May 13, 2021. https://www.azquotes.com/ quote/294073?ref=ants.

Brown, Brene. "The Research." Accessed May 13, 2021. https://bren- ebrown.com/the-research/.

Creswell, J.W. *Research design: qualitative, quantitative, and mixed methods approaches.* Thousand Oaks, CA: SAGE Publications, 2014.

Grant, Amy. "Apple Chilling Info: How Many Chill Hours Do Apples Need." Gardening Know How. Accessed May 13, 2021. https://www.gardeningknowhow.com/edible/fruits/apples/ chill-hours-for-apple-trees.htm#:~:text=Most%20apple%20 varieties%20need%20500,hotter%20summers%20than%20 other%20varieties.

Holm, Carl. "Ants lay trail to complex problem-solving." *ABC Science Online.* December 9, 2010. https://www.abc.net.au/ science/articles/2010/12/09/3089168.htm#:~:text=A%20spe- cies%20of%20ant%20could,than%20had%20previously%20 been%20thought.

NCSU WolfWare. "DDN 702 Research Paradigms in Design." Accessed May 13, 2021. https://wolfware.ncsu.edu/courses/details/?sis_id=SIS:2020:8:1:DDN:702:001.

TEDx Talks. "Weaver Ants, Problem-Solving, and Judgement | Jacob Wilde | TEDxQueensU," April 17, 2018, Video, 11:07. https://www.youtube.com/watch?v=Gg7EYOEYZ64.

The Nobel Prize. "Marie Curie Biographical," Accessed May 13, 2021. https://www.nobelprize.org/prizes/physics/1903/marie-curie/biographical/.

TH Trees. "Trees Through the Seasons." Accessed May 13, 2021. https://thtreeservices.co.uk/trees-through-the-seasons/.

CHAPTER NINE: BECOMING A NATURAL REFLECTOR

AnOther. "Alexander McQueen's Carved Prosthetic Leg." March 13, 2015. https://www.anothermag.com/fashion-beauty/7158/alexander-mcqueens-carved-prosthetic-leg.

BrainyQuote. "Zig Ziglar Quotes." Accessed May 14, 2021. https://www.brainyquote.com/quotes/zig_ziglar_617778.

Calaway, Libby. "The Catwalk Model Without Legs." NY Pos., May 25, 1999. https://nypost.com/1999/05/25/the-catwalk-model-without-legs/.

Gaille, Brandon. "19 Employee Motivation Statistics and Trends." Accessed May 13, 2021. https://brandongaille.com/17-employee-motivation-statistics-and-trends/.

Mower, Sarah. "Remembering the Potent Performance Art of Alexander McQueen's Collection No. 13—20 Years Later." *Vogue Runway.* September 14, 2018. https://www.vogue.com/article/alexander-mcqueen-no-13.

TED. "Aimee Mullins: Changing My Legs and My Mindset." February 1998. Video, 20:09. https://www.ted.com/talks/aimee_mullins_changing_my_legs_and_my_mindset.

TED 2009a. "Aimee Mullins: The Opportunity of Adversity." October 2009. Video, 21:42. https://www.ted.com/talks/aimee_mullins_the_opportunity_of_adversity.

TED 2009b. "Aimee Mullins: My 12 Pairs of Legs." February 2009. Video, 9:45. https://www.ted.com/talks/aimee_mullins_my_12_pairs_of_legs.

The Moth. "Aimee Mullins: A Work in Progress." December 6, 2010. Video, 12:09. https://themoth.org/stories/a-work-in-progress.

Verbruggen, Stijn. "Life is not a race." Pinterest. Accessed June 21, 2021. https://www.pinterest.ph/pin/505036545691100669/.